THE
RISE OF
ASHEVILLE

An Exceptional History of Community Building

MARILYN BALL

THE
History
PRESS

Published by The History Press
Charleston, SC 29403
www.historypress.net

Front cover, clockwise from top left: The YMI orchestra, 1908. *Courtesy of (p77.10.3.8.1a) Black Highlanders Collection, circa 1888–1972, D.H. Ramsey Library, Special Collections, University of North Carolina at Asheville 28804*; Hot air balloon. *Photo by Time Barnwell*; Savoy Café. *Courtesy of (N1264) E.M. Ball Photographic Collection (1918–1969), D.H. Ramsey Library, Special Collections, University of North Carolina at Asheville 28804*; Banjo player. *Photo by Tim Barnwell*; A glass vase. *Photo by Tim Barnwell*; Jackson Building, circa 1920s. *Courtesy of (N1232) E.M. Ball Photographic Collection (1918–1969), D.H. Ramsey Library, Special Collections, University of North Carolina at Asheville 28804*; Mural detail. *Courtesy of Kathy Triplett*; Downtown Asheville. *Photo by Tim Barnwell.*

Back cover, clockwise from top left: Fly fisher. *Courtesy of the Nantahala Lodge*; Sonny, Freakers Ball mascot. *Courtesy of Betsy Reiser*; Potter's hands. *Courtesy of Brian McCarthy*; Asheville mountains. *Photo by Jeremy Wilson*; A Ben Johnson glass vase. *Courtesy of Becky Anderson and the HandMade in America archives*; Electric streetcars. *Courtesy of (N1896) E.M. Ball Photographic Collection (1918–1969), D.H. Ramsey Library, Special Collections, University of North Carolina at Asheville 28804.*

First published 2015

ISBN 978.1.5402.0209.3

Library of Congress Control Number: 2015941627

CONTENTS

DEDICATION

In 2013, Western North Carolina lost a quiet leader with the passing of Bob Kelso, founder of Kelso Advertising & Design, an iconic Asheville-based ad agency serving this region for thirty-plus years.

Kelso loved the Western North Carolina mountains. Moving here in the late 1960s, he chose Asheville as his home—a place where he could be himself, do what he loved to do and serve his community.

Bob Kelso. *Courtesy of Marcia Kelso.*

I first went to work for Kelso in 1991, a time when the state map of North Carolina literally ended in Asheville, while the far western counties appeared as a vast wilderness with few roads or towns. For the next eighteen years, we worked together as partners. He was a mentor and a teacher.

His love of this region and his gift for design attracted him to the emerging tourism industry desperately in need of economic help to survive. There was not yet a room tax for hotels, so most rural counties had little or no money for exposure to the outside world, but Kelso believed Western North Carolina

Kelso offices from 1989 to 2009, Lexington and Walnut Streets, circa 1976–77. *Courtesy of (aap023) Asheville Area Photographic Collection, Southern Highlands Research Center & D.H. Ramsey Library, Special Collections, University of North Carolina at Asheville 28804.*

had the potential to be a major travel destination and could create a sustainable economy around the tourism industry.

A small group of visionaries and community leaders recognized a kindred spirit and asked Kelso to assist in leveraging the little money they had to invest in a marketing program. Understanding the power of collaboration to achieve a bigger goal, he helped reshape the area's tourism industry over the next eighteen years.

Kelso earned the respect of his peers, but what mattered most to him was the continued growth and success of his clients. His business model included acting with professional integrity, providing consistent results by partnering with his clients to understand their needs and developing cost-effective marketing solutions, regardless of budget.

His clients showed their appreciation for the personal attention and the quality of work they received by renewing contracts year after year. He had many clients for over twenty years, a statistic mostly unheard of for an ad agency.

Kelso understood the importance of creating partnerships by collaboration and cooperation, and he encouraged his clients to foster a model for working together versus competing with one another. Always open-minded, he was willing to try new ideas and listen rather than dictate. In this spirit, he helped the region slowly begin to emerge as the travel destination it is today.

He lived by the same values that brought so many of us here. He was a colleague, friend and mentor—and is the inspiration for this book.

FOREWORD

Since the first European settlers made their way into the southern Appalachian Mountains in the eighteenth century, Western North Carolina has been a land apart. Until the railroad was finished from Old Fort to Swannanoa after the Civil War, Asheville and the surrounding coves and valleys remained one of the most isolated regions in the eastern United States.

From that day to this, Western North Carolina has remained a place of great physical beauty combined with little commerce and less wealth. In 1904, when Horace Kephart was searching desperately for a blank spot on the map to retreat to during his famous midlife crisis, a place "back of beyond," he chose the high mountains west of Asheville because there were so few people there. Imagine a place, then, that has remained relatively isolated, a place that tourists love to visit because of its breathtaking beauty but a place where very few choose to remain because of its poverty. Only recently has Asheville—the small city in the center of the region—become a mecca for retirees and artisans, most of whom stay put, at least for three seasons of the year.

One of the results of Western North Carolina's long isolation is there exists a peculiar insider versus outsider view of the region and its people. For those whose ancestors have lived and mostly farmed in the mountains for generations—myself included—there is a fierce pride in who and what we are, a stubborn independence that can often get in the way of an evolving community. For those who come here seeking inspiration or peace in the southern mountains, there can be an equally determined impulse to improve the lot of the poor mountain folks, an impulse that can sometimes create more resentment than collaboration.

The wonderful thing about the stories Marilyn Ball tells in this book is they are peopled by natives and newcomers who reach across cultural and financial divisions that might have otherwise doomed their efforts. Men and women like Wayne Caldwell and Becky Anderson, whose families have lived and worked in the mountains for many generations, join forces with those who came here out of a genuine love for this place and its people. What is more, these natives and newcomers worked together to create real economic development in a crushingly poor region, without compromising the cultural riches that make this place unique.

My father, along with his brother and sisters, was born and raised in an isolated mountain cove. They had a saying that resonates in each and every page of this book: some of us were lucky enough to be born here; some of us were smart enough to come here. In each of these ten stories, those who were born here join hands with those who came here to create miracles of communication and community. May those of us who follow sustain what they started.

TERRY ROBERTS
Asheville, North Carolina
Author of *A Short Time to Stay Here*

ACKNOWLEDGEMENTS

I'd like to thank all the wonderful people who took the time to tell their stories of collaboration so I could share them with you. They all demonstrate how the power of a vision combined with dedicated action can change the course of history. These folks inspire me with their passion and determination in the face of daunting odds.

For Saving Downtown Asheville:

Wayne Caldwell, leader of Save Downtown Asheville, for the vision to mobilize business owners against the proposed downtown mall and the tenacity to show up at every opportunity to fight the forces determined to pursue a different vision for the city he loved.

Peggy Gardner, a student activist in college at the time, for her creative vision that led to "the Wrap," a public demonstration that was a first step in saving downtown Asheville from the mall project.

Jan Schochet, determined to protect the many family stores at risk, for her passionate and persistent resistance to the political forces behind the mall.

For Stone Soup:

Dick Gilbert, founder of Stone Soup and spiritual leader of Friends Enterprises, for his vision, belief in collaborative living and commitment to serving others as a way of life.

Carolyn Wallace, Stone Soup Friend and first director of the MANNA Food Bank, for her ability to inspire people and mobilize them to take action for a shared cause. With a heart of service, she brings her collaborative spirit to everything she does and teaches others to do the same.

For MANNA Food Bank:

Toby Ives, former director of **MANNA** Food Bank, for his ability to adopt someone else's huge vision and, with his common-sense approach and willingness to get his hands dirty alongside his staff and volunteers, take a growing organization to its full potential.

For HandMade in America:

Becky Anderson, visionary and the first director of HandMade in America, for her passion, inexhaustible energy and lifetime of service to others. Having grown up with respect for and dedication to the people of the mountains, she brings intelligence and heart to all she does.

For the River Arts District:

Brian and Gail McCarthy, founders of the Odyssey Center for Ceramic Arts, for sharing their stories and being a part of the creative movement that enabled our community to prosper and grow in the arts.

Kathy Triplett, a most gifted and talented artist, who made Asheville her home base and contributed to the collaboration of the River Arts District.

Trip Howell, owner of the Clingman Café, who serves up good food and provides a friendly atmosphere where artists and visitors alike can relax, enjoy the art on the walls and get to know one another.

Eileen and Marty Black, former owners of Cotton Mill Studios and strong advocates and major contributors to the River Arts District and its development.

Helaine Greene, who, along with her sister Trudy, rebirthed the Riverview Station into one of the pioneering properties in the River Arts District.

Rob Pulleyn, a visionary leader in our community, who, along with Kate Mathews, helped grow the arts community in Asheville.

Tim Schaller, owner of the Wedge Brewery, who is an advocate for the partnership between for-profit businesses and artists' studios.

For Smoky Mountain Host:

Mark Singleton, visionary leader and former marketing director of the Nantahala Outdoor Center (NOC), for his cooperative spirit and ability to help others put aside competition and come together for the good of all. While at NOC, Mark was a Smoky Mountain Host board member and a member of the North Carolina State Board of Tourism.

Betty Huskins, a community leader and consultant at Ridgetop Associates, for her vision and tenacity in fighting for the people of the mountains of Western North Carolina and helping them bring prosperity to the region.

For the Great Smoky Mountains Golf Association:
Brett D. Miller, former general manager of Cleghorn Plantation Golf and Country Club and advocate for the Great Smoky Mountains Golf Association, for his enthusiastic promotion of cooperation over competition and his ability to share his vision with others.

For the Blue Ridge National Heritage Area (BRNHA):
Jill Jones, director of marketing and communications, and Angie Chandler, executive director of the BRNHA, for their dedication to empowering people in the small towns of Western North Carolina to work together to preserve their natural and cultural heritage.

For the Family Store:
Jan Schochet and Sharon Fahrer, creators of the Family Store Project, for their determination to bring to light and preserve the contributions of Jewish store owners to the cultural and economic history of Asheville.

For YMI and The Block:
Darin Waters, an accomplished writer, educator and researcher, who kindly shared his knowledge and inspired us with his storytelling. His PhD focused on the post-emancipation experiences of African Americans in Western North Carolina.
Stephanie Swepson-Twitty, president and CEO at Eagle Market Streets Development Corporation, for her passion and vision for keeping the dream alive.

In addition, thank you to those who contributed to our understanding of the historical and cultural context in which these stories unfolded:
Betsy Reiser, a local business owner (Appalachian Realty), early entrepreneur and musician, who, with her special brand of enthusiasm, created many businesses to help bring new life to downtown Asheville.
David Cohen, artist, musician and humorist, who arrived in the 1970s, fell in love with the city and helped enrich it with his humor and his music.

Nancy Orban, former owner of High Tea Café, who provided a gathering place for the emerging community and supported the growth of a theatre and music culture in downtown Asheville.

Jean Wall Penland, artist and former member of the High Tea Café staff, who grew up in Asheville and joined with others who loved her city to serve the emerging community.

Joe Eckerd, visionary and business owner, who came to town in the 1990s and brought an entrepreneurial spirit and strong belief in collaboration to the business community.

Thank you for sharing your experiences and observations of the unfolding story of Asheville and Western North Carolina.

A big thank-you to my incredible team who helped usher this book into the world. There's an old saying about "hiring to your weakness," and putting together a book is a team sport! I so appreciate the watchful eyes and creative nature of those who went the extra mile to help. Thank you Kate Mathews, Deborah Morgenthal, Ginger Graziano, Sharon Oxendine and Jill Jones.

Thanks to Josh Awtry and Katie Wadington at the *Asheville Citizen-Times*, Ann Wright and Ione Whitlock at the North Carolina Desk of Pack Library in Asheville and Gene Hyde and Colin Reeve in Special Collections at D.H. Ramsey Library, University of North Carolina–Asheville, for help in finding historical photographs.

For additional help in collecting photos, thanks to Marcia Kelso, Betsy Reiser, Nancy Orban, Annie Martin, Dick Gilbert, Becky Upham (MANNA Food Bank), Becky Anderson, Brian McCarthy, Tim Schaller, Ken Abbott, Wendy Whitson, Del Holston, Jeremy Wilson, Annette Youmans (Nantahala River Lodge), Vicky Tingle (Springdale Country Club), Elly Wells, Kate Justus, Jan Schochet, Sharon Fahrer, Kathy Triplett and Tim Barnwell.

I am so fortunate to have such awesome friends. It's a great pleasure to have them along in my back pocket! Thanks all!

A special thank-you to Emoke B'Racz, founder and owner of Malaprop's Bookstore/Cafe, who helped pioneer downtown's revival and provides Asheville with a place where we can all aspire to be authors.

I'm deeply indebted to J. Banks Smither, my commissioning editor at The History Press, who recognized how special these stories are and gave me a chance to share them. Thanks, Banks, for being so encouraging, supportive and such a valued team player.

Thanks to Katie Stitely from The History Press for her patience and thoughtful advice as we worked through the editing process.

Many thanks to Terry Roberts, a true scholar and author, for reading my manuscript and providing such sincerity and insightfulness in the words that ultimately set the tone for the stories that follow.

Thank you to Betsy McClellan, for her continued optimism and support.

A very special and warm thank-you goes to my co-contributor and collaborator on this project, Pat Downing. Pat's professionalism, support, encouragement and friendship lifted me up at all times. Her endless enthusiasm and gentle ways warmed all who met with her to feel comfortable sharing their stories. Thank you, Pat, for all you've done for me.

And thank you, Asheville! When I came here all those years ago, this emerging town embraced me, and I am so grateful to be a part of a community that keeps on giving. It feels good!

Finally, a special thank-you to my family. My daughter, who was born and raised here in Asheville, is proud to tell people, "I'm a native." And so it goes...

Wall Street, circa 1970s. *Courtesy of the* Asheville Citizen-Times.

INTRODUCTION

It was, I think, the feeling of community when people came. It wasn't business as usual. Things were evolving... in an odd little way.
—Betsy Reiser

I can still see all the boarded-up buildings. They weren't boarded up when I was a child. There was such a nice downtown... It was really rather wonderful... We were in love with this place.
—Jean Wall Penland

In 1977, some friends and I wanted to be part of a sustainable community and live a life close to nature with people who had similar interests. When we discovered Asheville, we knew we had found our home.

The city was in decline, with most of the buildings boarded up, but there was something about it that appealed to us. There was a vegetarian restaurant on Market Street; a couple of food co-ops; a wonderful bookstore, The Captain's Bookshelf, on Haywood Street; and an entire street, Wall Street, with a little tearoom and bohemian-looking shops. There, we met some like-minded people, and we felt this place had a compatible community and unlimited possibilities.

We were part of an influx of people who came to this area to create a new way of life. Many of us had come of age during the Vietnam War, and we rejected the dominant philosophy of winning at all costs and the idea that some people have more value than others.

The opening of High Tea, 1974. *Photo by Bob Cain.*

We had lived through the peace demonstrations and the civil rights movement, and we saw our country reaching out to people in other countries through a new program called the Peace Corps. It felt like a new age. They were exciting times, and they taught us we were instruments of change and the future was in our hands.

Artists, entrepreneurs and off-the-grid homesteaders were settling in the Asheville area, and together, we created a new sense of place. Our intention was to create community—one that respected others and valued compassion, creativity and individual expression. We believed in cooperation and peaceful problem solving rather than win-at-any-price competition and winner-take-all.

Part of the appeal of this area was its rich agricultural heritage. We met and learned from those people whose families had lived here for generations and whose roots went deep into the soil of these mountains.

We saw beyond the stereotype of poor, backcountry Appalachian folk. We recognized, instead, people who were strong-willed, self-reliant and committed to living off the earth. They inspired us with the values and practices that had sustained them for generations, and we wanted that lifestyle for ourselves.

> One of the things about Asheville that I've noticed over the years is that this is a place where you can try anything. People come here and they say, "I want to start a cat grooming business." And there's no one here to say, "Well, don't do that."
> —David Cohen

We felt anything was possible. In the 1970s, few jobs were available, so newcomers had to create a way to earn a living. Some chose to live off the land. Some created businesses. With property values depressed, space was affordable, and slowly, a local economy reemerged. Our community grew organically. It also attracted some Asheville natives who shared our values and vision for the future. Together, we created a tribe of like-minded people that just kept growing.

As new people moved into the area, many were drawn to the emerging community. Over time, we came to be called the Asheville One Thousand. No one knows how many of us there really were, but we brought a new energy to Asheville and the surrounding area.

Most important to some of us was the emergence of a closely knit, vibrant and diverse community. Many came here for that purpose. No matter what we wanted for our own lives, we also wanted to create a better world, and we worked together to do that.

Entrepreneurs were created from the same mindset. People came with the intention of having a better life and being a part of something greater than themselves. They didn't necessarily intend to be entrepreneurs, but they wanted to serve the larger community. Some started out helping friends, and businesses grew to create products or services that people wanted. Others saw something that needed to be done, and they just did it, so nonprofit and service organizations came into being as well.

Businesses arose to serve the people—vegetarian restaurants, food co-ops, bookstores, theaters, music venues and dance halls. People created ways to get together, and in the process, they created a unique sense of place.

> Well, Appalachian Realty started in '79—because I didn't know any better...I didn't start out to make a business. I just started working with my friends and whatever, and it kind of grew.
>
> —Betsy Reiser

Sonny, Freakers Ball mascot. *Courtesy of Betsy Reiser.*

One of the first gathering places was a café on Wall Street called High Tea. It served light lunch and breakfast—baked goods, cheese, fruit, sandwiches and soup—and all kinds of teas and coffees. With tables inside and out on the sidewalk, it became a place where people got together.

There were art groups, writing groups, poets who sat in the corner and people who came in and told others what they had done that day. It was a stimulating place with impassioned conversations. Strangers who wandered in wondered what they had wandered into, but usually they came back for more. Musicians started hanging out at High Tea. They would play their music, and someone would pass the hat for them. They usually got free food as well.

After a while, a special theatre group, the Blue Plate Special, began performing there. It was irreverent, making fun of people and having fun in the process. That was part of the charm of that time and place—it was safe for people to be themselves. When Malaprop's Bookstore/Cafe opened in 1982, it became another gathering place for our growing community. The environment supported freedom of expression, and we would spend hours browsing the extraordinary selection of books, meeting with friends in the café, enjoying a good cup of coffee or maybe listening to someone read poetry.

With few restaurants in town, a potluck culture arose, which brought folks together to celebrate life or pursue a shared interest. Over time, more restaurants, health-food stores and food co-ops were created to meet the desire for fresh, local, healthy food.

People were having fun, and music was a big part of the emerging culture. Folks showed up at any venue offering music, and eventually, dance halls emerged, attracting people downtown as well.

A core value of the community was supporting one another. As a result, every music event, business opening and fundraiser brought a huge crowd. Posters went up at gathering places, so people stayed informed about what was happening. They were in it together. Any person who showed up at those events was considered a part of what we were calling the Asheville One Thousand.

The group had a vision of community and worked together, with one another and with the Asheville natives who shared our vision, to make it real. Gradually, the boarded-up buildings became home to new businesses, and people in the area

We began to find each other. What was there to do? Well, we'd have a potluck—no restaurants particularly...A lot of people played music and they got together, and I think it was a reemergence of the Farmer's Ball, which happened out in an old building that is still there on Warren Wilson Road...We'd go there, and it was square dancing and that kind of thing. You get to know a lot of these people, and it jells.

—Toby Ives

Wall Street, 1970s. *Courtesy of Nancy Orban.*

started to come downtown again. The central theme that arose was one of caring about others, collaboration and working together for the common good; it set the tone for the growth that followed.

Working together was a natural expression of the growing culture, and the stories in this book are just a small example of the many collaborations that contributed to the cultural and economic development of Asheville and Western North Carolina.

Saving Downtown Asheville tells the story of a small group of citizens who mobilized an entire community to prevent the destruction of eleven acres of the downtown area to make way for a mall. In the process, they preserved the historical heritage and unique charm of their city.

Stone Soup shows the power of coming together in community. A small group of visionaries with a commitment to positive social change started a business that became a gathering place for the larger community and provided a foundation for the natural food culture in Asheville.

MANNA Food Bank arose when a group of concerned citizens from across the region came together to address the issue of hunger, and over time, they engaged the entire community in providing the solution.

HandMade in America is an example of a more complex regional network of local collaborations that supports artists, stimulates economic growth through tourism and led to a more unified regional community.

River Arts District emerged slowly from deserted warehouses and factories and became a vibrant cultural and economic center for Asheville.

Smoky Mountain Host is an example of small businesses going beyond competition to work together for the good of all. With limited money, a clear vision and vast natural resources, these entrepreneurs created a marketing cooperative that increased tourism and stimulated economic growth in their region.

The Great Smoky Mountains Golf Association also embraced cooperation over competition, as golf club owners joined forces to promote their region as a golf destination, increasing financial success for themselves and their communities.

Blue Ridge National Heritage Area, another regional network of local groups, demonstrates the power of volunteers in small towns coming together to preserve their cultural and natural heritage.

The Family Store is a more personal story, as two young women worked together and found others who supported their project, to document and preserve an important part of Asheville's historical heritage.

YMI and The Block tells of a collaboration that led to the development of a community center that became the heart of the African American business community in Asheville.

For many years through my work with Bob Kelso, I was a participant in some of these collaborative projects. My responsibilities included providing direction and advisory support for the region's hospitality and tourism industry, including administration and execution of successful cooperative campaigns.

My eighteen years working with Kelso gave me the opportunity to live my passion—bringing people together and partnering in the most positive way. As a result, I found myself in the middle of the transformation of an entire region.

It really did take a village, not just to raise our children, but also to create the way of life we believed in. We found common ground and worked together. That was one of the keys to the success we have achieved in our region and the unique culture we enjoy today.

A few people with vision, determination and a belief in cooperation made a difference in their communities. Do you have a passionate interest? Are you looking for a way to solve a local problem or improve your community? Are you an entrepreneur trying to grow your business? My intention is to inspire you with these stories and encourage you to take the risk of reaching out to others—even those you may see as competitors—to work with them to create cooperative projects that will benefit all of you and enrich your community in the process.

>•<

I am of the opinion that my life belongs to the community, and as long as I live it is my privilege to do for it whatever I can.
—George Bernard Shaw

Beautiful downtown Asheville without a mall. *Photo by Tim Barnwell.*

1

SAVING DOWNTOWN ASHEVILLE

A Gift Wrapped for the Future

Two years ago, I was downtown and [a former supporter of the mall] came up and he said, "I just want to thank you. I was walking around and thinking, 'What would we be doing with a dead mall in the middle of town?' So thank you."
—Wayne Caldwell

Today, Asheville is a charming city nestled in the mountains of Western North Carolina. The people are laid-back and welcoming. The city is an architectural treasure, with dozens of carefully restored buildings dating from the early twentieth century. The downtown area is thriving, with art galleries, restaurants and shops drawing visitors from all over the world.

But it wasn't always this way.

Much of downtown Asheville would have been destroyed in the early 1980s were it not for a group of concerned citizens who valued their city and created a community-wide collaboration to protect it from the devastation of a major redevelopment plan. At that time, the city was in decline, but these volunteers believed that it could be restored and once again be a center of cultural and economic vitality.

A LITTLE HISTORICAL PERSPECTIVE

Asheville has a vibrant, prosperous past. The economic expansion during the first three decades of the twentieth century brought wealthy philanthropists and

> I do remember the very first thing that got me about Asheville was the downtown area—just the whole concise little pocket that it is—but with all this great architecture. It totally captivated me—and the fact that all those buildings were still there and hadn't been torn down.
>
> —David Cohen

talented architects to the area. Together, they created an interesting city center with a diversity of architecture and unique charm.

In the 1920s, the city expanded rapidly. People from around the country and around the world found their way to the area. The fresh mountain air was believed to be healing, especially for those suffering from tuberculosis or other respiratory problems. Asheville was in an economic boom.

But then, on November 20, 1930, the Central Bank and Trust went bankrupt. The county and the city lost most of their holdings, and by 1933, they were deep in debt. In fact, Asheville had the highest per capita debt of any city in the country. City officials vowed to pay off every cent they owed on their Depression bonds, and they did. It took forty-six years.

As devastating as this was for the residents of the area, ironically, it may have saved downtown Asheville. Other cities during the 1950s and 1960s were spending money on urban renewal projects, tearing down old buildings and erecting new, rather architecturally bleak replacements. But Asheville did not have the money to do the same, and as a result, most of the city's wonderful old buildings were spared. In the 1970s, a new suburban mall was built and many local businesses moved there, adding to the economic downturn of the central city. By the early 1980s, many of those buildings were in foreclosure or disuse.

THE CHALLENGE

To compete with the suburban mall, Asheville's city council decided to build a downtown mall. It planned to use eminent domain to tear down eleven acres in the heart of the city—including 125 businesses and two apartment buildings—believing a mall would revive downtown.

Some business owners in the area to be torn down agreed, believing the only cure was some form of urban renewal. Others saw that the destruction of those buildings would also destroy what was special about Asheville. They believed the downtown should be revitalized according to the city's official revitalization plan from the 1970s—through restoration of existing buildings.

> We felt taken advantage of, and if you feel taken advantage of, you've got to stand up for yourself and do something about it.
> —Jan Schochet

Passions were high on both sides.

Intent on saving their families' businesses, a small group of young people came together to stop the mall project. They knew the pro-mall forces had the advantage of money and support from powerful corporations and politicians, but they decided to leverage what they had—their passion and their ability to pull people together. Under the leadership of Wayne Caldwell, they created an organization called Save Downtown Asheville (SDA) to fight for their city.

Knowing the odds were against them, they began a grassroots campaign to inform area residents of what they were about to lose. When Peggy Gardner came up with the idea to create a visual representation of the targeted area, they enthusiastically jumped on the idea. They would wrap the perimeter of the targeted area in cloth.

The Wrap. *Photo by Annie Martin.*

❧·❦

"Do you have any idea how much fabric it will take to wrap eleven acres in the center of the city?" the man asked. "Two miles, approximately," he said.

The young volunteer swallowed hard, wondering if she was crazy to ask such a thing of the owner of the local salvage fabric business. But she accepted his offer to help with the project, not realizing the two miles of fabric would come in three- by five-foot sheets that would have to be tied together.

Volunteers worked through the night to create long ropes of fabric, and they were ready on the day of the demonstration.

❧·❦

The young people whose family businesses were in jeopardy reached out to the emerging community of newcomers, and two hundred people showed up to be part of "the Wrap." Volunteers formed a line around the area, holding the fabric border. It was a "Hands Around Asheville" moment. Some people jogged around the area, others walked the perimeter and the media covered the story. It was at once a festive and sobering event.

The Wrap was a success but only the beginning of the fight. Many people still remained unaware of what was at stake—not just those who lived or worked in town but also those from the surrounding area who saw downtown Asheville as their community base.

SDA continued to meet and to create ways to interrupt the city's plans. For over a year, SDA members wrote letters to the editor of the local paper. They attended every city council meeting, planning and zoning board meeting and economic development committee meeting. They didn't just show up. They did everything they could to disrupt the timetable—politely, most of the time, but persistently. It took determination, fueled by a passionate belief in their cause.

> When I studied the project map and realized how many of our favorite stores and meeting places would be obliterated—including the buildings where my father and grandfather had their shoe stores—I was astounded. I thought people needed some kind of visual reference, a history wake-up call. I'm glad my "Wrap" project drew some media attention and added to the fight against the mall.
>
> —Peggy Gardner

The Wrap in the news. *Photo by Annie Martin.*

The mall supporters were well funded, led by an ad hoc organization known as the Committee of 36, which morphed into Building a Better Asheville. It included the political establishment, the chamber of commerce and heads of every major corporation, including the newspaper, power company, TV and radio stations, Mission Hospital and the Merchants' Association.

SDA had a powerful adversary. Both groups spoke at civic organizations and advertised in the paper, fighting for the hearts and minds of city residents. It was a clear case of the establishment versus the little people, with an obvious contrast between the Committee of 36 and what some called the Committee of One Thousand.

Despite all efforts of SDA, the city proceeded with its plans. The planning and zoning commission passed a resolution declaring the area in question blighted. This allowed the city to proceed with its redevelopment plan, calling for the acquisition and demolition of the buildings in the area. To fund the mall project, the city had to issue a general obligation bond for $40 million, which required a public vote.

RECRUITING ALLIES

Realizing it needed all the help it could rally, the Save Downtown Asheville group reached out to the anti-tax folks in the community by creating a group called Taxpayers Against Bonds (TAB). The SDA members manned that office, organized a separate board of directors that included some well-respected anti-tax folks and led a professional-quality political campaign.

SDA and TAB were a coalition of two very different groups of people—those who loved downtown Asheville and those who might not have cared about downtown but who definitely did not want more taxes.

The last two or three months before the November 1981 referendum were hectic and intense. TAB raised thousands of dollars, which were spent on advertising and the logistics of getting people out to vote.

As part of the lead-up to the referendum, the city held a public debate. The anti-mall forces saw the value of that opportunity. They did their research, held rehearsals and showed up completely prepared. Over eight hundred people attended. The local television station broadcasted the debate live. No winner was declared, but the public was now more fully engaged.

SUCCESS

At the end of the day of the referendum, opponents of the mall gathered at a local restaurant, fully expecting the vote to go against them. Hundreds waited together for the results. When the TV cameras came in the door, a roar went up from the crowd. They had won. Some described it as David beating Goliath.

People power had prevailed over corporate power. A network of people who believed in community came together to support one another and fight for the future of the city they loved. When their way of life was threatened, they showed up and worked together to find a solution. By engaging others in their cause, they overcame their financial disadvantage. By creating a community-based collaboration, they were able to accomplish something nobody could have done alone. The historical heritage of downtown Asheville was preserved and, with it, much of the charm of the city.

> If it had been built, there would be little reason for people to go downtown. We would be nothing like we are now.
>
> —David Cohen

Putting Differences Aside

Eventually, some of the people from both sides came together to create the Downtown Association. Despite their differences, they chose to cooperate and work with one another and city officials to help Asheville grow and unfold into a vision city leaders had adopted years earlier, which focused on preserving the architectural heritage of the city.

Business and civic leaders worked together to take advantage of the designation of Downtown Asheville as a National Historic District, which made it eligible for private and federal grants to support their restoration plans. The city began improving infrastructure and restoring one neighborhood at a time.

As the future of the downtown began to look more promising, other people with vision and capital invested in the city. Together, they laid the bedrock for what Asheville is today. Along with the beautiful old buildings, a community came back to life.

Today, Asheville is a vibrant city with the second-largest collection of Art Deco architecture on the East Coast, second only to Miami. It is a treasure of architectural diversity. Because of the beauty of the downtown area and the diverse, creative local culture, Asheville has become one of the most attractive cities in the country.

⇒ ⇐

The Save Downtown Asheville years were worrisome on lots of levels. My greatest fear was that the bonds would be approved, the City would raze all those buildings and then the developer would walk away, leaving the fabric of our city with an incurable hole. Thanks to hundreds of dedicated volunteers, that did not happen, and we now enjoy as healthy a downtown as there is.
—Wayne Caldwell

⇒ ⇐

What We Learned

With creative ideas and commitment to a cause, a small group of volunteers can mobilize a community and change the course of history.

The reopening of Asheville Junction at the Biltmore Avenue location of Stone Soup, 1984. Pictured are Dick Gilbert (top) and Don Pedi. *Courtesy of the* Asheville Citizen-Times.

2
STONE SOUP

A Lasting Tribute to the Power of Community

*One of the goals we had was to create a real sense of community
among ourselves and to contribute to the larger community. I don't think
growing up in our culture prepares us for cooperation/collaboration,
for deep listening to other people, for caring as much about what
other people think and need and feel as what we need and think and
feel. Collaboration is a way of being that needs to be learned over a
period of time—and there has to be a real commitment to it.*
—Carolyn Wallace

In 1974, the buildings on the campus of Allen High School, formerly
a boarding school for African American girls from Asheville and the
Carolina mountain region, were standing empty and useless. It took
a visionary with a commitment to service to stir the pot that became
Stone Soup.

➳ ⬿

*It's a Wednesday morning, and a truck backs up to the loading dock of the cafeteria of the
old girls' school. A young couple hop out, their jeans and sneakers still muddy from their
foray into the fields of a local farm. In the rear of the truck, cardboard boxes are laden with
fresh vegetables bound for the tables at a little collectively owned restaurant, Stone Soup.*

*Inside, the Friends are already bustling about the kitchen, preparing food from
scratch—soups, rolls, breads, desserts and salads for the first salad bar in Asheville. At*

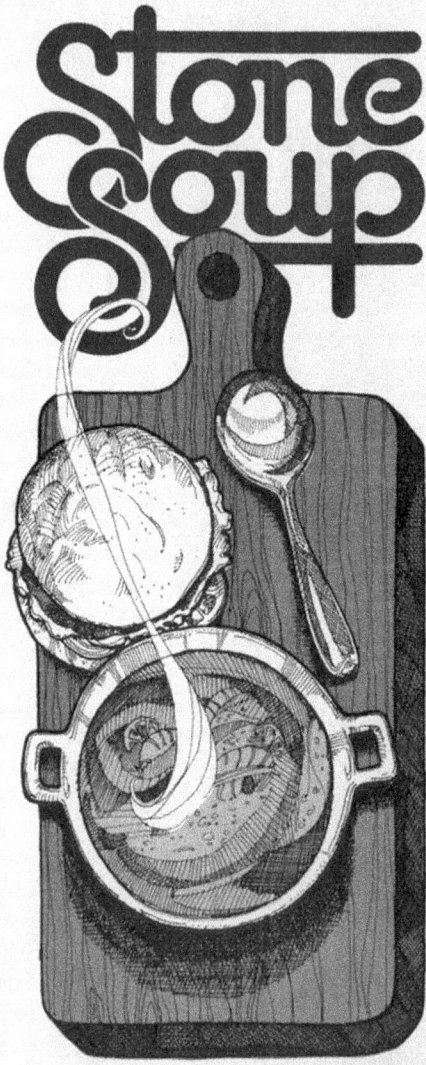

Stone Soup logo. *Courtesy of Richard Gilbert.*

lunch, many people who work for the nonprofit organizations now housed in the renovated buildings will gather to eat and socialize.

Stone Soup is the heartbeat of a change steadily coming to downtown Asheville.

❧ ❧

The former school, closed in June 1974, was owned by the Women's Division of the United Methodist Church and operated by the National Division of the United Methodist Church. Dick Gilbert, an ordained Methodist minister, was asked to suggest other uses for the buildings.

A survey of community ideas turned up a possible use of the buildings as a low-cost home for nonprofit agencies and also as a base for the church's own program for young people. To financially support this enterprise, Gilbert proposed a worker-owned business on campus that would provide funding to support the complex and offer additional services to the community. The women's and national divisions enthusiastically endorsed his vision. Not only did the church make the buildings available for the project, but it also offered the services of five young volunteers in the church's US-2 Program, similar to the Vista Program of the United States.

The original staff of ten called themselves the Friends. They shared a clear desire to create a sense of community among themselves and to contribute to the emerging larger community. They all received the same salary, there was no hierarchy in the group and decisions were made by consensus. The Friends researched the current living wage and set that as their salaries. Thus began Friends Enterprises.

The empty buildings at the Allen Center became the home of a co-op

> The same people were in the line every day, and they became your friends.
> —Jan Schochet

of nonprofits. A number of agencies relocated there, including the United Way, Family Services, the Community Relations Council, the Boys Club and the Agricultural Extension Service. The center also provided a home for the Children's Grammar School, as well as a day care and family life education program operated by the YWCA. The city schools eventually adopted the latter as the Asheville Alternative High School.

Agencies were able to keep expenses low since nobody was making a profit off the rent they paid. Because the agencies were located in the same area, they also benefited from the cross-fertilization of ideas that can happen when people are in close contact. The Friends created a collectively owned and operated business and transformed the school dining hall and kitchen into a little restaurant called Stone Soup. First, it was just to give the people who worked at the Allen Center some place to eat lunch.

The food, all made from scratch, was high quality and inexpensive. Soon, Stone Soup's reputation for good food also drew customers from downtown and the surrounding area.

People came for the food but returned time after time for something more. The round tables seated eight to ten people, so diners ended up sitting with people they didn't know. Workers came from their jobs downtown, women dropped in before or after shopping, parents who had dropped their kids off at school or day care stopped in for a meal. It became a gathering place for people across socioeconomic lines, a place of true community. In fact, it became a go-to place to have a good lunch or to meet friends or strangers.

Stone Soup had a lasting effect on the region. Its fresh, local food appealed to the growing number of people who wanted to eat more responsibly, and it introduced others to a healthier way of eating. As time went on, the Friends supplied their homemade bread and alfalfa sprouts to local grocery stores and restaurants and grew strawberries and other produce on a local farm, laying the groundwork for the farm-to-table and local food movements such as the Appalachian Sustainable

> If you were interested in the arts, there was one place to go for music—the Asheville Junction at Stone Soup. Everybody went there.
>
> —Betsy Reiser

Agriculture Project (ASAP) and Slow Food Asheville, which links the pleasure of food with a commitment to community and the environment.

The region now abounds with locally owned organic farms, farmers' markets, whole food stores and restaurants serving up the kind of homegrown food products that brought Stone Soup its fame.

But that's not all! Early on, Stone Soup became a gathering place for local musicians, who created a wonderful folk tradition called the Asheville Junction. On weekends, musicians and music lovers from all parts of the region came to Stone Soup's Asheville Junction to share and enjoy a rich mixture of contemporary and traditional mountain music.

BEYOND STONE SOUP

> We all came from a space within ourselves of commitment to be a part of positive social change. We wanted to create community for ourselves and be a part of creating community in the larger sense. We were grateful to find others with the same values and ideals.
>
> —Carolyn Wallace

In addition to Stone Soup, the Friends used profits from the restaurant to bring other ideas to life at the Allen Center. Motivated by a belief in ethics, fairness, sustainability and the importance of taking care of one's neighbors on an everyday basis, they helped staff and fund a children's shelter for kids in emergencies. That program, called Our Place, later evolved into Caring for Children, a nonprofit agency that is still providing services to children, teens and families in the Asheville area.

Dick and Mary Gilbert's home became another place for children in foster care to go, especially those who were difficult to place. Assisted by other Friends, this low-profile program cared for twenty-six young people over its four-year life.

The Friends created a teenage telephone hot line called Huckleberry, named for that famous alienated youth. Stone Soup provided a part-time staff person who trained young volunteers to be peer counselors. From their office in the Allen Center, the volunteers provided a listening ear and talked with callers about drugs, pregnancy and other problems facing troubled teens. The program ran for three years, with the hot line helping the callers but also giving the peer counselors experience in active listening and talking with people struggling with serious problems.

There was also a quiet side to the work of the Friends. With their support, a staff person lived in the neighborhood adjacent to Stone Soup and worked to help

Stone Soup logo. *Courtesy of Richard Gilbert.*

its disadvantaged residents figure out how to help one another. One of the Friends described it as "grass roots being a good neighbor." Over time, a new neighborhood council participated strongly in designing its own future in the face of public urban renewal efforts.

The community was not the only beneficiary of the work of the Friends and Stone Soup. The staff members who shared the difficult work of keeping an active restaurant going developed into a strong support group for one another. Their consensus process of decision-making engendered a deep level of respect for and loyalty to one another and an understanding of and commitment to the idea that collaboration leads to greater good than the work of any one individual. Their experience had a long-lasting effect on the Asheville area. As time went on, the original members of the collaborative moved on to new endeavors; many went into other service professions. Dick and Mary Gilbert continued as worker-owners of the restaurant and as caregivers for kids who needed a place to live.

The ethics and guiding principles of Stone Soup—living a life of meaning and purpose—continued to inform its decisions and led to its ongoing contributions to the larger community. The restaurant continued as a worker-owned business. Through the years, it provided work, skills training and a community of support for many people who were in transition.

Stone Soup continued to be a favorite meeting place in Asheville for seventeen years (from 1977 to 1994), moving over the years to the Manor Inn on Charlotte Street, then to Broadway (the current site of Mellow Mushroom) and then to Wall Street (the site of Early Girl Eatery).

By 1994, downtown Asheville was emerging as a vibrant community, and as other restaurants appeared on the scene, Gilbert decided to close Stone Soup. He continued to influence the local food scene for more than a decade with his worker-owned Blue Moon Bakery on Biltmore Avenue, which closed in 2005.

Working daily at the arts of community and collaboration as applied to a business setting, we became increasingly convinced that enabling others to use those skills/values in ordinary business practice could make a real contribution to social and economic justice in the workplace.

We saw Stone Soup not only as a basic human service but also as a living and learning experiment in enabling ordinary workers to have a real voice and vote in their workplaces. We even hoped that others could learn from our experience. We may never know if anyone did, but that dream was certainly worth the hard work we applied to it.
—Dick Gilbert

What We Learned

A small group of people with a commitment to positive social change can combine business and service to others and, in the process, enrich their community.

3

MANNA FOOD BANK

Feeding the Hungry in Western North Carolina

Why food banking works is because you have poverty and you have wealth, and you bring the two together.
—Toby Ives

In those days, we didn't have any money for anything like marketing. It was go and talk to groups, go to the Rotary Club, go to other civic organizations, go to churches when we could get invited and try to get the word out that way. It was really community building at the grassroots level.
—Caroline Wallace

In the early 1980s, one out of five children in North Carolina did not have enough to eat. Many of them lived in the Asheville–Buncombe County area, and their need was the catalyst for a new community collaboration. No one knew anything about developing a food bank, but as more local people became aware of the hunger in their midst, people from churches, civic groups and nonprofit agencies came together to create a solution. They joined under the leadership of such agencies as Asheville Buncombe Community Christian Ministries (ABCCM), Eliada Home for Children, the Junior League of Asheville and the Hunger Awareness Group. Out of this collaboration, MANNA Food Bank was born. It was a hands-on, roll-up-your-sleeves response, entirely dependent on volunteers.

Fun times volunteering. *Courtesy of MANNA Food Bank.*

❊ • ❊

It's drizzling as the truck pulls up to the warehouse. Eight people scurry out to the truck. Two men begin to hand boxes full of cans to the line of volunteers, and soon the day's haul is safely out of the rain.

Inside, the boxes are lined up on long tables, and five people are busy sorting the contents into other boxes. As those get filled, two men place them on a handcart and push them into the next room. A young woman is standing at the large industrial sink, washing off cans that are sticky or dirty.

At the other end of the building, six people are pushing grocery carts and selecting items from among the cans and boxes on the shelves. A distinguished-looking woman is sitting by the door, waiting to help the next "customer" check out.

None of these people are getting paid, except in the knowledge that what they are doing is important to the families of Western North Carolina.

❊ • ❊

MANNA Food Bank was launched in 1983 in the basement of an old building at Eliada Home for Children, rent free. Bob Lawrence Power Equipment donated a hand truck to move pallets, and MANNA was ready for business.

MANNA had a dual purpose: get good food that would otherwise be wasted to people who really needed it and help businesses avoid wasting food.

The project got off to a slow start. The first director, Carolyn Wallace, had no paid staff. She depended on the cooperative efforts of volunteers, people working for organizations that would benefit from the food and others in the community who cared about hunger issues. The McClure Fund offered the services of its secretary for fifteen hours a week during the first couple of years, and the Red Cross offered office space, which made a big difference to the fledgling organization.

> People care about kids, and they don't want kids to be hungry. To the degree that we were able to help that awareness become more pervasive, it helped to bring people out. It was very much a one-on-one kind of effort in terms of building the community of people who were aware and cared and wanted to do something about it.
>
> —Carolyn Wallace

Board members and staff met with business owners in the food industry to convince them to donate food they could not sell—for cosmetic or other reasons unrelated to food value or safety—rather than throwing it away. Bell Sysco and Asheville Showcase supported the effort by donating equipment.

During those early years, the food bank could not have survived without support from Second Harvest, the national network that enabled food banks to share excess food with one another. As members of that grassroots network, MANNA staff and volunteers also learned the food bank ropes.

Gradually, local business owners responded to requests for donations and began contributing larger amounts of food. But the biggest boost came when Ingles, a local grocery chain, entered into a mutually beneficial partnership with MANNA.

MANNA GOAL NUMBER ONE: GET GOOD FOOD TO PEOPLE WHO REALLY NEED IT

From the beginning, in order to reach those in need, MANNA set up a distribution system. Day-care centers, food pantries and nonprofits that had a food component could become members of MANNA. They received food from the bank for a minimal per-pound contribution. This income did not begin to cover the cost of the food, but it did help to defray the handling cost and provided a baseline for MANNA's future fundraising efforts. A family in need was never charged or expected to donate for food received.

MANNA GOAL NUMBER TWO: HELP BUSINESSES AVOID FOOD WASTE

In the grocery business, when products arrive damaged, manufacturers buy them back, reimbursing stores for transport and processing expenses. If one item in a shipping box is damaged, the entire carton is often sent to a reclaim center. Ingles, one of the area's major grocery stores, had been paying a company to process the damaged goods. Since most manufacturers did not want the items back, the company had been discarding most of them.

MANNA applied for and won the contract to run the Ingles reclaim center, a step that gave it access to much of the food that was being discarded. In

Helping our community is rewarding. *Courtesy of MANNA Food Bank.*

turn, the innovations MANNA management put in place the first year of operation increased Ingles's income from vendors by more than $1 million. During the first year, MANNA staff scanned 650,000 items a month for 8.9¢ each, and with a computerized system, they were able to provide Ingles with an accurate accounting of every item. MANNA also kept all the items that did not need to be returned or discarded, which dramatically increased its food supply. Today, Ingles is still a primary supplier.

RAISING THE MONEY TO FEED THE HUNGRY

When Toby Ives became the next executive director, he knew his biggest challenge was raising money to support and continue to expand the program. MANNA had moved into a much larger space and had grown to include 150 member agencies throughout the western part of the state. But most people in the area still did not know about the program, and people don't contribute to what they don't know about.

To increase MANNA's exposure, Ives organized a gourmet breakfast. Board members invited church and civic leaders to enjoy Eggs Benedict and learn about the program. He asked the 125 attendees to go back to their churches, clubs or businesses and tell at least 10 people about the importance of the work MANNA was doing.

Word spread, and as the network of supporters expanded, so did the financial contributions. As the program grew, MANNA needed to upgrade its warehouse. A local philanthropist led the capital campaign, and he encouraged several of his friends to meet with food bank staff to learn more about the program.

❧ ❧

A woman in a linen suit steps out of her BMW and enters the warehouse. A man in jeans and a T-shirt approaches her. "Can I help you, ma'am?"

"Yes. I'm looking for the director." The man turns and points to his right. "That's him over there. We just got a delivery of sweet potatoes this morning."

Turning, she sees a man with a push broom sweeping sweet potatoes scattered on the floor into a pile, while two other men are scooping them into burlap bags.

"Which one?" she asks.

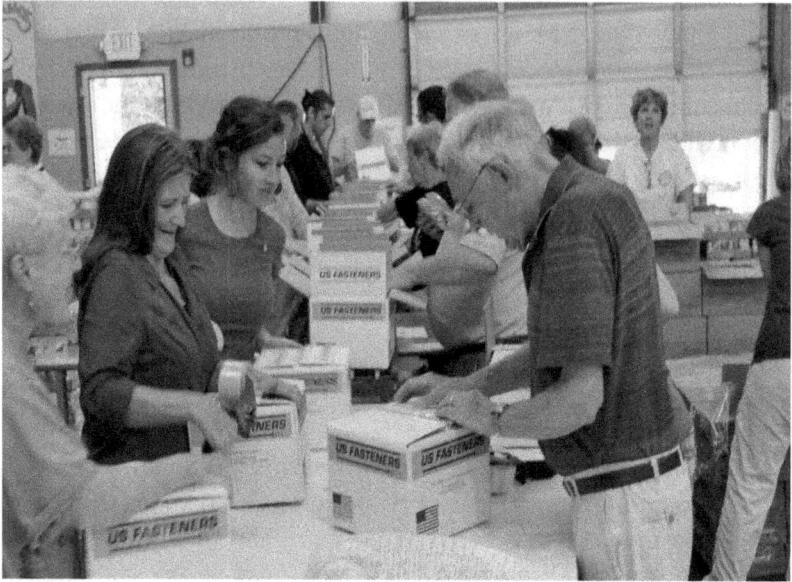

Making a difference for others. *Courtesy of MANNA Food Bank.*

"*The one with the broom,*" *he answers.* "*Whenever there's work to do, he's right in the middle of it.*"

The woman smiles. "*I'd like to meet him,*" *she says.*

Toby Ives puts down his broom and wipes his hands on his jeans before shaking the woman's hand. They talk for a few minutes, and then he takes her on a tour of the warehouse.

He does not learn until later that she had decided to donate $100,000 for the new warehouse. "*I knew I was going to donate,*" *she told a friend later,* "*when I saw the director pushing a broom.*"

❦ ❦

The campaign was a success. Large donations came in from local businesses and philanthropists, and MANNA was able to upgrade its facility and expand operations. The growth of the program was the result of contributions, large and small, from an army of supporters over many years. Today, the MANNA Food Bank network includes churches, businesses, nonprofit agencies and thousands of individuals.

Each year, MANNA sponsors fundraising events and food drives that enable the food bank to distribute food to over 220 partner agencies in sixteen counties. As a member of Feeding America, MANNA is part of a national network that links together 205 food banks in the United States.

Hunger is still an issue in Western North Carolina—a complex and challenging issue. MANNA Food Bank continues to work to educate the community about issues of hunger and poverty, to save food that would otherwise be wasted and to assist its partner agencies in Western North Carolina in their work to help alleviate hunger and malnutrition.

›• ‹

Never doubt that a small group of thoughtful, committed citizens can change the world; indeed, it's the only thing that ever has.
—Margaret Mead, anthropologist

›• ‹

WHAT WE LEARNED

A small group of concerned citizens can take the first steps in addressing a community need, recruit volunteers to help and, over time, create a solution that involves the entire community.

I used to say there are four steps in food banking, and you could say they are the steps in a lot of nonprofits:

Step one is to recognize there are people thinking, "There's food going to waste over there and hungry people over there and so what—I'm going to go play golf."

The second step is kind of where I was initially—"Let's get the two together."

The third step is to invite those who are being served to your own table for first serving. Let's not separate ourselves.

The fourth step is to continue working toward a society in which the people we now serve have both the comfort level and the resources to invite us to their table.

—Toby Ives

A Cherokee basket. *Courtesy of Becky Anderson and the HandMade in America archives.*

4

HANDMADE IN AMERICA

Creating a New Paradigm for
Economic Prosperity

*In Appalachia we had been told for so long: "You're so dumb, you are
so stupid, you are so poor, you will never be..." and we bought into it
for so long—we let people do that to us. That day is over... I think we
are extraordinarily resourceful... I call it the genius from the dirt.*
—*Becky Anderson*

Western North Carolina is a mountainous region dotted with small
towns isolated from one another and from the outside world.
These towns grew up as the early homesteaders came together to create
communities. Most of them are home to talented artists and crafters who
work at home or in schools and sell their products through galleries or
local arts fairs. But living and working in rural mountain towns has its
economic challenges.

In 1993, Becky Anderson was serving as the director of economic
development for the Asheville Chamber of Commerce when she became
aware that a grant from the Pew Trust might be available to help bring about
civic change in these rural areas. She and a group of visionaries applied for
and received a $400,000 grant and got started on a new project to expand
the economies of these areas of the Western North Carolina mountains.
The project would be called HandMade in America, and its goal was to
work at the grassroots level to stimulate economic growth—focusing on the
local artists—and create a more unified regional community.

It was a crazy idea. And at first, it was not embraced by all.

≫• ≪

It's just before seven o'clock, and people are engaged in heated discussion as they enter the town hall. Inside, they have split into two camps—those in favor of the tourists coming to town and those opposed. Tension fills the air.

As the mayor begins to speak, the noise subsides. He introduces the out-of-town speaker, and the woman seated in the wooden chair next to him slowly stands and looks out at the audience. She reflects for a few moments, introduces herself and then surprises them with a question: "What are the sacred places in your town?"

People in the audience look at one another and then back at her. After a long silence, a man in the back of the room speaks up, "Well, our church is sacred." A murmur of agreement passes through the room.

A woman shouts out, "And the cemetery." People nod and begin to speak out.

"Don't forget the spring."

"What about the garden path by the lake?"

Soon, they're all talking at once. Then, as the talking subsides, they look around at one another.

The speaker smiles and thanks them and then asks another question. During the next hour, they talk about places in town where they don't want visitors to go and the things they are proud of in their town that they do want visitors to see.

The speaker thanks them again for their input and explains that they are in charge of how they participate in the program. "You are the most important resources of this town," she says. "It's all up to you."

As the meeting closes, people linger to talk with one another. On his way out the door, an older gentleman looks back and says, "We should send them to the old oak tree, too."

"Yeah, it's a beauty," someone replies.

≫• ≪

Becky Anderson is a gentle persuader. She became the first director of HandMade in America and galvanized people in small towns throughout the mountains by bringing them together in meetings like the one described above. The collaborations that were formed have dramatically changed the entire region.

To begin the extensive implementation process, the HandMade staff visited every town that invited them and held a public meeting to explain the program. Sometimes two people showed up; sometimes twenty-two came. In Cherokee, everyone—the tribal council, tribal members, even children and dogs—showed up.

PLANNING FOR SUCCESS

Over four hundred people from eighteen counties participated in the planning process. They came from town and county governments, the banking community, nonprofit agencies, galleries, gift shops and the craft community.

The planners were divided into four teams: economics, education, cultural and tourism. They met twenty-two times in twenty-two different towns. Most team members had never been to the other towns represented, so through the planning process, they had a chance to see and appreciate the uniqueness of each community and to begin to work together as a region.

Since most participants did not know anyone from the other towns, HandMade staff created a process that provided opportunities for

The art of pottery making. *Courtesy of Brian McCarthy.*

them to develop new alliances. The planning sessions included breakfast and lunch. Participants were not allowed to eat with anyone from their own hometown, so they got to know their regional neighbors. They discovered others with the same interests, and they often found partners in other communities for their individual projects.

After agreeing to be a part of the regional plan, each town did an assessment of its resources—human, cultural, economic, historic and natural—and then developed local projects. This process required a collaboration cluster that included a town official, crafters, educators, shop owners, representatives from a local bank or nonprofit agency and someone from the tourism industry.

Together, they developed the local information to be included in a new guidebook to help attract visitors to their towns. When the local plans were complete, HandMade in America published and sold *The Crafts Heritage Trails of Western North Carolina*, which described eight driving loops in Western North Carolina with five hundred stops. It detailed the work of each artist

> People are their own best resources—this is what we were for. All projects had to be community based. Everybody came equal to the table. That's how we got started and how we got the plan put together.
> —Becky Anderson

and listed times they were available for visitors to see them craft their products. It also included restaurants, inns, bed-and-breakfasts and other points of interest in each area.

Many communities wanted to promote not only their arts and crafts but also the farms and other businesses that supplied the artists with their raw materials. Some towns also offered lovely gardens and natural trails, an important part of the natural heritage of the area. So a short time later, HandMade in America published a second guidebook, *Farms, Gardens and Countryside Trails of Western North Carolina.* That book took the adventurous tourist down "back roads and scenic byways to some of the most beautiful farms and gardens of the Blue Ridge Mountains." Offering a different focus, it attracted even more visitors into the region.

Getting Ready for Visitors

Many smaller communities needed help preparing for visitors, and they wanted to improve their towns in other ways as well. To meet those needs, HandMade staff created the Small Towns Program for towns with populations of fewer than two thousand. They provided technical assistance and training, and each community developed its plan and created the partnerships needed to implement it.

The Results

Craft became a significant growth industry and a draw for tourists, one of the region's main sources of revenue. In 1995, an economic impact study determined that the impact of the craft industry on the region was $122 million. In 2008, a second survey showed that, with over four thousand craftspeople in the region, the economic impact of craft in Western North Carolina had grown to $206.6 million.

There was also a cultural impact. With the dramatic increase in craft tourism, people from within and from outside the region developed a greater understanding of the local craft heritage. By visiting the artists and seeing the creative process, visitors could appreciate the skill, time and effort involved.

Crafts came to be seen as a substantial asset in the region. Several communities developed hands-on workshops, residencies and mentoring programs that transformed the region's craft heritage into valuable educational tools for school-aged children. Artists worked with faculty to design creative projects that met both academic and cultural goals.

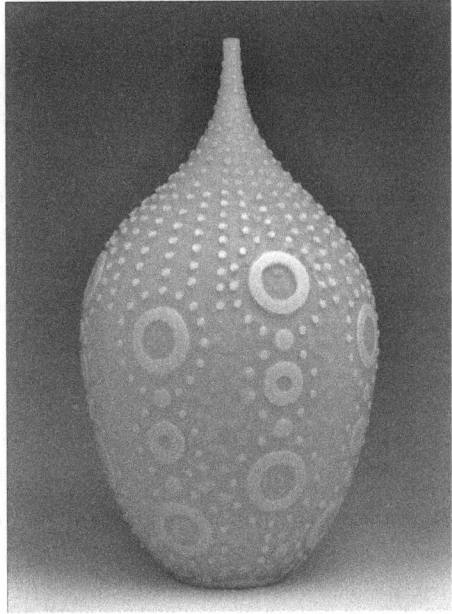

A Ben Johnson glass vase. *Courtesy of Becky Anderson and the HandMade in America archives.*

A lesson about pottery glazes became a chemistry project, and a quilt demonstration also taught geometry. These programs help to preserve the craft heritage while providing students opportunities for creative expression.

The entire process empowered local townsfolk to have a say in their communities in a way they had not before. Working together to create a vision and implement it, people strengthened personal and community relationships.

A New Regional Identity

Perhaps as important, the Small Towns Program helped create a regional identity and a sense of cohesiveness among towns that were previously disconnected from one another. There was a new awareness of belonging to the larger region, and partnerships and friendships were forged across town and county lines. For instance, after two of the towns in the program experienced horrific, destructive floods, they reached out to their new partners for help. People came from all the other towns in the program and helped wash windows, pick up trash, paint and whatever else needed to be done. Another case in point of the cohesiveness formed in the program: when the North Carolina Rural Center wanted to take the small-town model statewide, it got funding from the legislature and offered grants to small towns. The communities in the Small Towns Program refused to compete against one another for the money, and eventually, the state created a shared grant so they could apply together. As loyalties grew stronger, people started going to one another's weddings, funerals and other celebrations. They had truly become members of a regional community.

HandMade in America Today

Twenty years after its inception, HandMade in America's legacy in the region lives on. Its award-winning programs helped leverage public, private and community resources to grow the economic impact of the region's craft industry. Although the organization closed in July 2015, it will always be the cornerstone of many lasting friendships throughout the region.

❧ ☙

Do community first, and economic development will follow.
—Becky Anderson

❧ ☙

What We Learned

When people come together to solve problems that matter to them or to create something of value to their community, they will step up, speak up and come up with solutions.

GUIDING PRINCIPLES OF HANDMADE IN AMERICA

- Recognize craft as an integral part of economic development and see the creation and appreciation of the handmade object as transformative to individuals and communities.
- Recognize that people in communities serve as the best resource to understand their challenges and opportunities and to seek and find solutions.
- Include everyone who wants to participate in the process.
- Use a regional approach, bringing together individuals and organizations from different communities in cooperative partnerships.

SMALL TOWN PROGRAM GUIDELINES

In order to participate in the program, a town had to agree to:
- select a local planning team that included at least five people, one of whom was a town official
- meet three times a year to learn the skills they needed to accomplish their local objectives, such as how to do a town assessment, write grant requests, manage a project, designate a historic site or develop a trail or a river walk
- share with each other lessons learned—what worked and what didn't
- develop a mentoring relationship with another town and visit each other
- come to the aid of any town in the program if there was an emergency such as a flood
- chip in and help—not with tax dollars but through fundraising— if any town could not raise the match money for a needed grant

Asheville Cotton Mill (rear), 1976. *Courtesy of (aap048) Asheville Area Photographic Collection, Southern Highlands Research Center & D.H. Ramsey Library, Special Collections, University of North Carolina at Asheville 28804.*

5

RIVER ARTS DISTRICT

A Community of Artists Emerges from Deserted Remnants of a Bygone Era

It's amazing how much change in the community is initiated by a few really forward-thinking people who have gone out on a limb.
—Kathy Triplett

In the late 1970s, what is today a vibrant artist community and a major attraction for Asheville residents and tourists alike was a collection of deserted, rundown factories and warehouses. The transformation of the area along the French Broad River into what is now the thriving River Arts District is a testimony to the power of vision, perseverance and cooperation. The result is a thriving community of artists and an economic center for Asheville and the region.

❧ ❦

The students file into the classroom, uncertain of what to expect. They speak softly among themselves as they sit at the long tables and look up at the young man who will be leading them on their creative journey. This is a beginners' ceramic art class.

In front of each student is a lump of possibility in the form of gray clay.

"Don't be afraid of the clay," the instructor says. "You're in charge. Just have fun with it."

Following his lead, the students tentatively begin to squeeze the clay. Someone giggles and then others follow. Soon, laughter fills the room. The creative process is in full swing. At this time, none of them realize just how much this journey is about to change them.

➽ ⬿

Brian and Gail McCarthy moved to Asheville in 1979. Brian, a potter, found a place to set up his wheel in an old, converted mica plant on Thompson Street along the Swannanoa River called Highwater Center. This mostly undesirable location appealed to a few local artists who needed inexpensive space for their studios. Rent was cheap since the factory was no longer being used. Brian settled in and became part of a small group of artists.

Back then, a big challenge for ceramic artists was finding good-quality clay. No suppliers were located near Asheville, most produced only small quantities and the quality of the clay was questionable. These challenges led Lawrence Bradshaw, another potter at Highwater, to mix his own clay. Soon he was selling to other potters. As the demand for clay increased, he purchased a commercial dough machine, capable of mixing 250 pounds of bread dough. With this increased capacity, he was able to offer clay to more ceramic artists.

To supplement his income, Brian McCarthy began working part time for Lawrence in the clay business. That increased his exposure to other potters and gave him the opportunity to learn the complicated business of making clay. When Lawrence joined the Peace Corps nine months later, the McCarthys bought the business from him, including the dough mixer, five tons of raw materials and a list of fifty customers. This was the beginning of Highwater Clays.

Clay mixing is a complicated art. As a potter himself, Brian understood the importance of producing high-quality clay for ceramic artists. This involved mixing different clays from different parts of the country and processing it to meet the requirements for different types of pottery and sculpture. To support his customers, Brian sought out better prices and reliable quality supplies. He slowly learned the ins and outs of the clay production process through experimentation and networking with others in the business.

While Brian struggled to learn the clay business, Gail worked in the local tourism industry to supplement their income. The clay business grew steadily, and eventually, they outgrew their Thompson Street location. In 1985, Highwater Clays leased a ten-thousand-square-foot warehouse at 292 Riverside Drive. With quality products and good customer service, the company continued to grow steadily over the years. By investing all their profits back into the business, the McCarthys were able to hire more employees and invest in bigger and better equipment, including a stainless steel hamburger mixer they found in Pennsylvania.

Brian and Gail also wanted to support their customers by expanding their services to include ongoing educational opportunities. There were very few classes for potters and sculptors, so the McCarthys invited guest artists from around the country to teach workshops in Asheville. This provided an opportunity for the artists to increase their skills and network with one another, and as word spread, attendance increased.

> We always had the idea of learning more ourselves and helping the community to have the opportunity. There weren't many workshops around.
> —Gail McCarthy

A Vision of an Artist Co-op

It was challenging to find space for the increasingly larger classes, but Brian and Gail saw their customers as a community of fellow artists, and they wanted to support them whatever way possible. They recognized the value of support from others who understood the artistic journey.

They had a vision of a permanent place for artists to gather. In their wildest dreams, they could envision a co-op for ceramic artists where they could produce their art, continue to increase their skills and sell their products. But at that point it was just a vision; they had no idea how to make that happen.

Fast-forward to 1994

Gail was looking for a larger space to use for storage of their supplies, and she came upon a group of old buildings for sale.

"When I walked into 238 Clingman Avenue, the building looked at me and said, 'I'm not a storage space, I'm a store.' Then I went into 236 and it said, 'I'm not a storage space, either. I'm a school.' So I went back and told Brian, 'You have to go look at that space and see what it tells you.' When he came back he said, 'That's not a storage space. That's our store and our school.'"

Now Everything Changed

We have an area where the creative process is not only very accessible and doable. It's encouraged as a good thing.

—Trip Howell

After about the second or third class at Odyssey, it really took hold of me. I still remember having my hand on a slab of clay, and I knew that I was supposed to be doing this. The whole process of starting with something wet and soft and then firing it and it coming out hard and dry. It was wonderful.

—Rob Pulleyn

So the McCarthys purchased the four adjacent buildings, 236–242 Clingman Avenue, and began to transform them into their long-dreamed-of store and school. After updating the electrical and mechanical systems, they installed new sidewalks and renovated the interiors.

The 236 Clingman Avenue address became Odyssey Center for Ceramic Arts, with individual and group workspaces for potters and sculptors and plenty of room for classes and workshops. The McCarthys had envisioned a place where artists could gather and learn from one another, but they also wanted to encourage the public to experience the satisfaction of working in clay. Finally, their dream had come true.

As Odyssey Center evolved, it provided private and shared studio space. Don Davis, the first school director, offered a regular series of classes, as well as special workshops. When he introduced an eight-week summer program taught by guest ceramic artists, artists showed up, professional and amateur, from around the country.

While the McCarthys were on their personal journey, the area around them was gradually coming to life. Artists from outside the area began applying for the few resident artist positions. In exchange for a studio with twenty-four-hour-a-day access and free firing, each resident artist worked an eight-hour shift each week, helping with the operation of the center.

Studio Stroll

Over time, the small community of artists began to coalesce. Wanting to promote their art, they explored ways to show the public what they had to offer. They promoted themselves with the first Studio Stroll—a public tour of the working studios. It was a small beginning, but it laid the groundwork for what has become a highly acclaimed semi-annual event.

The informal collaboration of artists grew with each year. During those early years, the public was reluctant to venture into an area full of old, dilapidated warehouses and factories, but as the number of artists increased, so did the number of visitors.

> It was never intended that it be our River Arts District. We don't like to take ownership over things and to tell people how they're supposed to do things. We like that concept of nurturing something and then letting it go—tossing it and saying—"OK, it's your turn now."
>
> —Gail McCarthy

Within the next few years, several artists purchased nearby buildings, and many more studio spaces became available.

NOW IT'S OFFICIAL

As the community of artists grew, their informal collaboration was not addressing other challenges facing them. The district was not known to most of the general public and was essentially invisible to tourists passing through. If people did attempt to find it, they often got lost on the way, and those who stumbled on it could not find the art studios because most of the buildings had no signs of any kind.

> We wanted the artists to be able to afford to be there, and we wanted to build the district so that it would be for working artists' studios. There's nothing else quite like it in the whole country.
>
> —Eileen Black

A small group of leaders emerged and began meeting to create a more formal structure, and in 2003, River Arts District Artists, Inc. (RADA) was born. The group's first objective was to draw more visitors to the studios. It created a quality color brochure for the next Studio Stroll and set out to rebrand the area as the River Arts District.

Now, as a legal entity, the artists had more of a voice, and they began to use it effectively. They made sure they were represented on the chamber

Northlight Studios, formerly a tannery curing facility. *Courtesy of Wendy Whitson.*

Wedge Brewery and Studios, formerly a produce and livestock distribution center. *Photo by Ken Abbott.*

of commerce, and they got the City of Asheville to officially recognize the area as the River Arts District and install directional signs that led visitors to the area.

> You see the trolleys that come down to the River Arts District full of people? Why are they coming here? They're getting off to see the art.
> —Trip Howell

They knew the building owners and the artists themselves had to create a welcoming atmosphere that would invite visitors to stay. It didn't take much encouragement, and soon every building with studios had a building name sign and a big Welcome sign. Their efforts paid off. The Studio Stroll brought more people than ever, and the RADA board decided to expand the stroll to two days twice a year.

Another focus of the board was supporting the artists in creating successful businesses. They brought in accountants, bankers, lawyers and others who could help familiarize them with some of the tools and skills they might need to succeed financially.

A significant development was the opening of Clingman Café at 242 Clingman Avenue in 2005. Now, the artists had a place to get a cup of coffee or a light lunch. People came together who otherwise had been just passing each other on the street, which added to the feeling of community that had been growing among the artists. Visitors were welcome, and it gave them a place to stop and get a meal before continuing their tour of studios. It wasn't long before the café became known as the living room of the River Arts District.

Over the years, membership in the RADA increased dramatically, and the River Arts District became a desirable address. Other businesses came to the area, including several restaurants. Today, the RADA membership has grown to well over 150 artists, representing studios in twenty-four buildings.

What began as a collaboration of artists working together to support one another has become a larger cooperation of artists and other business owners to preserve the essence of the River Arts District while managing the evolution of the area to meet the demands and opportunities of the future. It is community building in progress, and many of the current leaders in the RAD community—artists and business owners alike—have the vision and the wisdom to work toward the future as a unified group.

≫• •≪

When we were first shown the property as a potential site for our candle manufacturing back in 1990, I remember feeling the excitement of the past industrial vibrancy of the area. The building was mostly empty, and it echoed inside. It was surrounded by a chain-link fence with barbed wire, but you could feel the energy of all the industry and creative energy that took place here long ago, and we wanted to be a part of it.

At that time, we had no idea we would someday own this beautiful building and help transform that past industrial and creative energy into the vibrant creative collaborative community it is now. There are so many lives we have touched and who have touched us as well. It's been a true gift and honor to be a part of the process of creating opportunities and connections and the transformation of Riverview Station and the RAD.
—Helaine Greene

≫• •≪

What We Learned

Sometimes collaborations grow organically as people follow their own path and reach out to help others along the way.

6

SMOKY MOUNTAIN HOST

We're Part of the State, Too

*We knew that it made a lot of sense to promote the region as a
destination rather than promote it on the strength of a single entity.
That's just not enough to draw someone for a multiday experience.*
—Mark Singleton

THE CHALLENGE

As late as the early 1990s, on most maps of North Carolina, the state
seemed to end at Asheville. The far western counties showed up as
wilderness areas, as if the many small towns and the Cherokee Indian
Reservation did not exist.

Those counties make up almost 60 percent of the Great Smoky
Mountains National Park, the most visited national park in the United
States, and include the original homeland of the Eastern Band of Cherokee
Indians. The region is the premier outdoor watersports recreation area in
the southeastern United States. It also offers hiking, camping, train rides,
horseback riding, gem mining, golfing and some of the best trout streams in
the nation.

The small towns that dot the region are known for their unique downtowns,
offering world-class crafters along with rich cultural music venues, historic
bed-and-breakfasts, restaurants, hotels and gift shops. However, since there

The beautiful Blue Ridge Mountains. *Photo by Del Holston.*

The Cherokee Indian Reservation is home to the Eastern Band of Cherokee Indians. *Photo by Jeremy Wilson.*

was not yet any "room tax" or other public money in the region to support tourism marketing, each business was on its own.

In those days, North Carolina officials marketed the state as a whole but seemed to lean toward the urban areas and the beaches. Since Asheville was the only urban area in Western North Carolina, it seemed a daunting task to level the playing field.

THE RESPONSE

To address this challenge, in 1987, a small group of business owners, along with the local chambers of commerce and the Eastern Band of Cherokee Indians, joined forces to create Smoky Mountain Host of North Carolina, a 501(c)(6) nonprofit organization encompassing the seven far western counties of North Carolina and the Qualla Boundary (the Cherokee Indian Reservation). They knew there must be a creative way to leverage what they had—a limited amount of money, a vision and one of the most beautiful natural settings in the country—to become a vibrant tourism destination.

※ ※

It's dark when they climb aboard the Cherokee Boys Club motor coach, and many are unsure of their chances of success. It may be a long shot, one of the travelers who owns a whitewater rafting company thinks to himself. But he looks around at the county commission chairs and the chief of the Cherokee, sees determination to match his own and decides it's at least worth a shot.

None of the riders is experienced in talking with a governor, but by the time they arrive in Raleigh, they have their strategy laid out to ask him for a first-time-ever visitor center not on an interstate highway. With heads high and a sense of pride in their beautiful mountain region, they step off the bus and head for the governor's office with a singular goal in mind—presenting their vision for the future of tourism in the far western part of the state and securing the governor's support and funding for a public-private partnership.

The room is packed when they make their proposal to Governor Jim Martin, and you can feel the tension in the air. However, no one expected what was to come next. At the conclusion of the presentation, Governor Martin looks over at his secretary of transportation and says, "Find the money. This is something that North Carolina needs to do."

The business owner smiles as he drinks his coffee and reads the headlines in the Asheville Citizen-Times the next morning. "Governor Martin Pledges to Build Visitor Center in Macon County on US-441." It certainly was worth that long shot, he thinks. Who would have thought it would really happen?

⇶ ⇷

That was only the first of many successes for the Host—a regional visitor center that would refer tourists to their businesses. The region already consisted of several major attractions, such as the Nantahala Outdoor Center, Ghost Town in the Sky, Oconaluftee Indian Village and the outdoor drama *Unto These Hills*, but the attractions had never been marketed collectively as a destination. The Host members decided to leverage financial resources to find and market to a larger audience by providing a venue for a multiday vacation. In other words, tell the larger story of this beautiful vacation destination to travelers.

The idea was good on paper, but putting it into action required a mind shift among local chambers of commerce and attractions that sometimes saw their neighbors as competitors. The other challenge was the North Carolina Division of Tourism, which traditionally focused on other regions of the state. The Host group succeeded in recruiting businesses and organizations by showing them that there was strength in numbers and that it was smart business to work together. The foundation of the organization was cooperation, as in cooperative advertising—pooling money and promoting everyone. It was a success from the beginning.

The central group of the Host collaboration was the marketing committee, made up of member volunteers and representing diverse segments of the community. They met monthly and made decisions about how best to spend the collective advertising dollars.

GAINING INFLUENCE

With these initial successes, the Host leadership set its sights on what the members considered their share of state tourism money. A few of them stepped out of their comfort zone and successfully lobbied to become members of the North Carolina Travel and Tourism Board. Having started out to persuade the powers that be, they actually became part of the power structure.

Winter fishing. *Courtesy of the Nantahala River Lodge.*

Now having a voice at the table, they helped put together a cooperative advertising program at the state level, matching what they were doing at the regional level. The message of collaboration and cooperative marketing started to define the tourism industry on a statewide basis.

As a result, the AdvantageWest Economic Development Board made money available for marketing. The Host received $50,000 annually to be used for promotion of the region, which provided a big incentive for local businesses to join the Host group and participate in its cooperative marketing effort.

With economic development dollars paying part of the advertising costs, Host member businesses could then buy into the ad campaigns targeting their specific audiences. For every dollar they put in, they received three dollars and up in media exposure, ultimately attracting more visitors to the region.

Membership brought several other benefits. Each member was listed in the *Smoky Mountain Host Visitor Guide*. The annual meetings provided an opportunity to learn about current trends in the tourism industry and

Smoky Mountain Host exemplifies the worth of collaboration and leadership for the good of all. The public-private endeavor to build a regional visitor center has served as a cornerstone for the robust regional tourism industry in the North Carolina mountains.
—Betty Huskins

continued to provide ways to leverage resources. Over time, the members developed personal relationships and a strong regional pride.

Smoky Mountain Host covers the seven western counties of North Carolina. Two other Host groups—Blue Ridge Mountain Host and High Country Host—serve the central mountains around Asheville and the northern mountain area.

These collaborative efforts paid off. Tourism increased dramatically in the entire region, and businesses flourished—not only at tourist attractions but also at hotels, bed-and-breakfasts, restaurants and other businesses in various segments of the hospitality industry. More jobs were created, and the tax dollars generated provided greater economic impact for the region and the state.

Through their collaborative efforts, the Host members branded the North Carolina side of the Great Smokies as a desirable destination for travel. Individual businesses, talking with their own voices, could not have had the same impact. Most people think in terms of where they've been and not where they could be, but these visionaries saw a greater possibility, and they had the courage to make it happen. In the process, they helped grow an entire region that had once been overlooked.

※·※

These folks all had a business interest—they all had skin in the game. There were outside resources that we could leverage. There were people that had a vision for how that could work. Behind those individuals, there were followers—that's what it takes. Those three things combined to make a core program that could be successful.
—Mark Singleton

❯❯·❮❮

WHAT WE LEARNED

With a vision and a shared goal, businesses choosing cooperation versus competition can increase success for themselves and even transform a region.

Golfing in Western North Carolina. *Courtesy of Springdale Country Club.*

7

THE GREAT SMOKY MOUNTAINS GOLF ASSOCIATION

Playing a Round Together

It was formed to get more of "Let's complement rather than compete, bring them to this region, get on the same team."
—Brett D. Miller

THE CHALLENGE

Golf courses in the mountains of North Carolina are reminiscent of the sport's origins in the mountains of Scotland, providing players some of the most beautiful scenic courses in America. And yet, in the 1980s, the dozens of courses in Western North Carolina competed for players, mostly locals—and none was doing very well. Until one day, a bizarre idea took hold—cooperation among the courses and a marketing strategy that would attract more players to them all.

❊ ❊

The weather is less than perfect—overcast, with a chance of rain in the forecast. Last year, this would have been a disaster for this mountain golf course, but today, as the owner looks out over the greens, he sees that the early birds are already at it, the ones who like to get in their rounds and end with lunch and a beer at the nineteenth hole.

Looking across at the parking lot, he can see a steady stream of new arrivals. Never in his wildest dreams had he believed that partnering with his competition could mean business in November.

※ ·※

In the 1980s, when many golf enthusiasts were taking golf vacations, places like Southern Pines and Myrtle Beach were flourishing, while the harder-to-reach, less well-known courses nestled in North Carolina's mountains and foothills languished. With golfers preferring to travel to a single destination that offered several courses within an easy drive, the region was ideal, but players simply didn't know about it.

Having small marketing budgets, these golf clubs did not typically advertise out of their immediate areas. They depended on a primarily local market, which comprised too few players to sustain the number of courses.

THE RESPONSE

The courses struggled until the advent of a unique partnership—the Great Smoky Mountains Golf Association. In 1989, local golf clubs took a step toward collaborative marketing, and as a result, they put Western North Carolina on the map as a golf destination.

Initially, many golf club owners resisted the idea of cooperating with competing golf properties for a limited share of the audience. Soon they realized they could work together and actually attract more golfers to the area. By offering up a golf buffet with plenty of choices, they would all have an increase in visitors.

The key to this successful partnership was a coupon book that was sold at member golf courses, welcome centers in the region and the Asheville Chamber of Commerce. For $150, the purchaser received two green fees for each course in the book. With that incentive, golfers began to play all the courses they had paid for instead of just their local clubs.

In a cooperative marketing effort, the coupon books were advertised nationally in publications such as *Golf Digest* and *Golf Magazine*, media that had never been affordable to any single course. By pooling resources, these beautiful mountain courses gained the attention of a much larger audience.

Greens with a view. *Courtesy of Springdale Country Club.*

The member courses made their contribution to the association marketing budget by selling the coupon books in their communities. In return, they got a lot more visitors. Although they gave up some green fees, they still received cart fees and income from meals and accessories, so the additional visitors generated significant revenue for them.

SUCCESS

The coupon books sold out quickly, as local golfers discovered a way to get more rounds for less money, and many people bought the booklets as stocking stuffers for their favorite golfers. Out-of-towners discovered a new golfing destination and began enjoying the beauty and laid-back way of life in the mountains.

As new golfing tourists came into the region, other businesses also benefited. People came to town to play golf, but they also needed gas, food and sometimes a place to stay overnight. Taking advantage of being in a new place, they visited local shops and points of interest. In time, many golfers relocated to the area, so this collaboration, designed for the financial success of the individual members, had a far-reaching effect on the entire region.

Today, golf is an important component of tourism in Western North Carolina, a testament to the power of cooperation over competition. Playing a round—together. Fore!

⇛•⇚

Many times over the years, I have heard of people who were introduced to this area on a golf package and said, "Wow! That is beautiful. We want to move there."
—Brett D. Miller

⇛•⇚

WHAT WE LEARNED

Despite initial resistance to a new idea of working with competitors, people will get on board when they see the benefits for everyone.

8
BLUE RIDGE NATIONAL HERITAGE AREA

Widening the Scope of Regional Partnerships

*Getting people talking was probably the biggest challenge,
but it's also the biggest blessing of the whole thing.
—Angie Chandler*

E arly collaborative efforts laid the groundwork for a larger, twenty-five-county regional initiative aimed at uniting the people from this vast and rural mountain area. As a result, in 2003, the U.S. Congress and the president of the United States awarded the eleven thousand square miles of North Carolina's mountains and foothills the designation of a National Heritage Area. This honor recognized the region's unique natural and cultural landscape and its significance in the history of America. This would not have happened without collaborations among many people and groups, not only in Asheville but also in towns and counties throughout Western North Carolina.

※ ※

"I think we can do this, people," the woman leading the group says. "But it's not going to be easy. We're all going to have to work together to get this legislation passed."

"Ha!" a young man laughs. "Good luck on that."

"But, Brian, you've seen what's happened here in Asheville with collaborative efforts." The leader levels her glance at the naysayer. "You wouldn't be here if you didn't get that."

The Stoney Creek Boys, a fixture on the Shindig stage since 1963. Shindig on the Green in Pack Square Park, Asheville, 2010. *Photo by Tony Martin.*

Brian's face begins to turn red, but he doesn't reply.

A man wearing the uniform of the National Park Service speaks up: "Well, for my part, I see the value in trying to create a National Heritage Area, not just for Asheville but for all of Western North Carolina, especially those communities adjacent to the Blue Ridge Parkway." He, too, glances at the young man and then turns his gaze to the leader. "What do you need from us?"

"Commitment," she replies. She looks around the room. "From all of us in this room, from our business partners, our legislators, our national parks, everybody."

"And from the people who live here," another in the room speaks up.

The leader grins and gives a short sigh. "Yes. Especially from the people who live here. And yes, I know they haven't always played nice, some haven't even played together at all. As I said, this isn't going to be easy. But I'm asking those of you who have taken time to come to this meeting, can you commit to the work that it's going to take to create a new National Heritage Area for Western North Carolina?"

She looks from one to the next in the group who have come to the meeting. One by one, they nod. Then her gaze falls on the red-faced young man. "What about you, Brian?"

He grins sheepishly. "I get it. I'm in."

❧ ❦

The process of developing a feasibility study for becoming a National Heritage Area began with the cooperation of several individuals who were key players in other collaborative projects: HandMade in America, Smoky Mountain Host, the North Carolina Arts Council, AdvantageWest Economic Development Group, the Eastern Band of Cherokee Indians and the National Park Service (Blue Ridge Parkway).

> Well, no matter where you're going in your future, you always have some seed from the past.
>
> —Angie Chandler
>
> Our job was bringing people together.
>
> —Jill Jones

The area is noteworthy for its natural beauty, Cherokee and early American cultural history, world-renowned hand craftsmanship, vibrant musical heritage and a traditional agricultural way of life. Now, as a National Heritage Area, the region receives federal funding to support the planning and implementation of local and regional projects to preserve that heritage, tell its stories and use these heritage assets as a foundation for economic development.

To address the issue of lack of communication among counties, communities and even citizens of the same town, the newly formed Blue Ridge National Heritage Area (BRNHA) Partnership—with the support of AdvantageWest, the region's economic development commission—organized county heritage councils composed of volunteers. These stakeholders came from different sectors of the county—elected officials, community leaders and people involved in education, tourism, arts, historic preservation and land conservation. These local groups became both the backbone and the heart of the Heritage Area.

A new partner in this effort was the Tourism Division of the North Carolina Department of Commerce, which assigned personnel, known as heritage tourism officers, to aid in this grassroots effort. They, along with others, facilitated meetings at which everyone had a chance to present ideas.

❧ ❦

"There are sandwiches, soft drinks and cookies over there." The group leader invites those in attendance to the county library meeting room to have a bite of lunch as the discussion gets started.

It's a diverse group—some from the tourism industry, a representative from the North Carolina Agriculture Extension Agency, a greenway project coordinator, the county Arts Council director, an apple grower, a professor from the local community college—people who don't have a lot in common individually but are curious about this new thing called a National Heritage Area.

The leader, a young man with a tendency to blush, does the usual "around the table" introductions, and as the meeting proceeds, ideas are shared and new understandings are formed. At the end of the day, a list of their county assets is written in red marker on large paper sheets hanging around the room. Business cards are exchanged. A game plan for moving forward is in place.

When the last person has left the room, the young man picks up his cell phone and dials the main office. "Hey, this is Brian," he says. "Listen, I owe you an apology. I never thought I'd see it happen, but these folks can work together."

≫ ≪

> We think in those terms [economic value], but it could be social value—it could be a lot of different types of value. But it had to be of value to a group…It's the fabric of our lives. It's our history…and our future.
>
> —Angie Chandler

Assigned the task of completing a thorough inventory of their cultural, historical, natural and recreational resources, these councils met regularly for a few years. Some are still active. Some have evolved into other community improvement groups.

Once the inventory was complete, each heritage council developed a list of all the projects it wanted to implement to "preserve, interpret, and develop" its local heritage resources. The process brought people together and helped them find ways to cooperate on projects supporting their mutual interests and to improve their communities.

People who once did not talk or support each other's projects were now seeing the value of working together. It was the Blue Ridge National Heritage Area initiative, however, that got these conversations started.

From these inventories of hopes, dreams and realities, the BRNHA staff clearly understood the direction being given by stakeholders throughout the region. From this base of information, they compiled a comprehensive management plan, which was required by the federal government to guide the organization in its work.

A rich history and culture on the Cherokee Indian Reservation. *Photo by Jeremy Wilson.*

These county heritage plans also gave organizations the opportunity to apply for **BRNHA** grants to support many projects locally and regionally. The millions that have been awarded in hundreds of grants have generated new heritage tourism products, tourism promotion, farmland and agricultural promotion, small town improvements, establishment and support for the Junior Appalachian Musicians afterschool education program, barn quilt trails throughout the region and much more.

> It's very important to have expectations that are realistic and not pie in the sky and not let enthusiasm overwhelm the reality.
>
> —Jill Jones

The funds received from the federal government through the National Park Service must be matched dollar-for-dollar by money from other sources, which has encouraged counties, communities, civic organizations and others to invest in heritage projects in their own backyards. In fact, partnerships among local organizations have been key in the success of grant applications, as public tax dollars are leveraged, bringing additional financial support to projects and programs throughout the region. In McDowell County, for example, the county and school system partnered to provide matching funding for a BRNHA grant to restore the barn at the Carson House, one of the county's heritage sites. The barn, now a museum exhibiting antique farm equipment, has become a teaching tool for the school system where children can learn about a nineteenth-century farm. The project was successful, partly because of the BRNHA grant, but more so because of the community partnerships that worked together to make it happen.

A High Tide Raises All Boats

The Appalachian Sustainable Agriculture Project (ASAP) is one of many programs that received seed money from the BRNHA and then went on to obtain funding from other sources and become a major player in the region. Today, ASAP is helping to support the agricultural community throughout the entire region.

Museums in Partnership, a loosely structured affiliation of nearly one hundred large and small museums in Western North Carolina, evolved out of the planning process for the county heritage plans. Facilitators recognized that these mostly small, independent museums shared common challenges and brought them together to collaborate on ways to address their needs. This collaboration costs no money and only requires a little bit of time. It is driven by the passion of the people involved, museum professionals who now share ideas, resources and knowledge.

A recent partnership between the BRNHA and the North Carolina Arts Council is the Blue Ridge Music Trails of North Carolina initiative. Western North Carolina has a national reputation as a music-rich region, and its traditions of old-time string band music, ballad singing and bluegrass are internationally renowned. The Blue Ridge Music Trails project aims to tell this story, build attendance at festivals and venues and help the state of North Carolina claim its significant contributions to American music. It is expected that, over time, the project will also strengthen the economic value of this heritage sector.

The folks in the North Carolina mountains have a long and proud history. They value their culture and the natural world that has sustained them for generations. When asked to come together to find ways to preserve that heritage, volunteers showed up and discovered how much they could do in partnership. Their efforts have transformed their communities and the region.

A view of Shindig on the Green in Pack Square Park taken from the top of the Jackson Building, Asheville, 2010. *Photo by Jerry Nelson Photography.*

❧ ❦

In the very early days, the Heritage Area organized county heritage councils. I was involved to a degree in that—getting together volunteers from all the different sectors of the county, like the county manager and the arts council and the museums and the conservation people and the outdoors people. All these people before that had been very separate in their goals—this is my deal, my money, don't you touch it—very territorial. And we were very successful—it took a while—in getting the players to the table and they kind of got the bigger picture: if we all work together, then we can all succeed.
—Jill Jones

❧ ❦

What We Learned

When given the opportunity, people at the local level are the ones most likely to create solutions to best serve their communities.

The Mission of the Blue Ridge National Heritage Area

To protect, preserve, interpret and develop the unique natural, historical and cultural resources of Western North Carolina for the benefit of present and future generations and, in doing so, to sustain our heritage and stimulate improved economic opportunity in our region.

GUIDING PRINCIPLES FOR
LOCAL HERITAGE COUNCILS

Participants were asked to agree to certain principles that support good decision-making. Those agreements included:
- active listening—really hearing what everybody is saying
- respect for everyone at the table
- treating everyone at the table as an equal
- welcoming all ideas
- agreeing to make decisions for the good of everyone

GRANTS GUIDELINES

According to the federal mandate, the grants must support at least one of five North Carolina mountain heritage themes on which the designation was based: agriculture, crafts, music, nature and Cherokee heritage. Higher value is placed on projects that:
- are regional or involve more than one county
- involve collaborations among organizations
- leverage financial matches from project participants and other grantors

Carmichael Drug Store. *Courtesy of (N1876) E.M. Ball Photographic Collection (1918–1969), D.H. Ramsey Library, Special Collections, University of North Carolina at Asheville 28804.*

9

THE FAMILY STORE

Collaboration Preserved Asheville's Jewish Heritage

No one can do anything by themselves. You talk to people and they might say, "Well, talk to so-and-so." One person will tell you two people's names and each of them will tell two more. Then you've got this giant thing going on.
—Jan Schochet

Growing up in a family business and as a member of the Asheville Jewish community, Jan Schochet was aware of the history of Jewish-owned family stores in Asheville. Her paternal great-grandfather and his brother had come to Asheville in 1887. From her own family stories and those of others, she knew of the rich history of Jewish business owners who had helped shape the culture in Asheville.

With a strong sense of social responsibility, Jewish entrepreneurs had made significant contributions to Western North Carolina through donations of time, money and other resources. Many had been active in civic organizations and had taken leadership roles in the community. For decades, they had been an important part of the social and economic structure of the city.

When Schochet learned of an online archive about "all the different groups living in Western North Carolina," she was surprised to find "African Americans in WNC," "The Cherokee in WNC," "The Scots-Irish in WNC" and even "Hillbillies in WNC" but no "Jews in WNC." She was troubled by the lack of information about the history of her family's culture.

With a master's degree in folklore, she had done extensive research on disappearing cultures, and she realized this culture—her own—was also endangered. Unlike previous generations, young people were choosing not to go into their family businesses. Time was running out—many of the store owners who had inherited stores from their parents were in their eighties. Their personal stories would be essential to understanding that history.

BRINGING OTHERS ON BOARD

> Find others who share your interest and go out and do it.
> —Sharon Fahrer
>
> Realize what your strengths and what your weaknesses are and bring on people who have your weaknesses as their strengths to balance you.
> —Jan Schochet

When Schochet met Sharon Fahrer, she found a partner who shared her interest in Jewish history. With a master's degree in urban planning, Fahrer was used to working on collaborative projects. In 2001, when they decided to do a project together, they formed a company, History@Hand, to let people know about this untold piece of Asheville history.

The North Carolina Humanities Council awarded them a planning grant that enabled them to bring together eight scholars from around the state, comprising historians, an economist, an archivist and a historic preservation consultant. The planning team advised them on a direction for the project and how to write grant proposals to fund it.

Then, as a result of talking with a lot of people they thought would be helpful, Schochet and Fahrer were able to narrow their focus. They decided to interview as many Jewish store owners and their families as possible in order to capture their family stories.

In the process, partnerships emerged, including the Southern Jewish Historical Society; Public Interest Projects, Inc.; University of North Carolina–Asheville; and University of North Carolina–Chapel Hill. The North Carolina Humanities Council funded the oral history collecting. Pack Library and UNC-Asheville loaned them recording equipment, and the Center for Jewish Studies at UNC-Asheville gave money to the library archives to digitize the information they collected. The Center

The Family Store: A History of Jewish Businesses in Downtown Asheville, 1880–1990. Copyright History@Hand; courtesy of Jan Schochet and Sharon Fahrer.

for Diversity Education provided a digital camera to record interviews, and in return, History@Hand helped it by including questions in its interviews for a Library of Congress World War II oral history project that the center was conducting.

GOING TO THE SOURCE

Over a two-year period, Schochet and Fahrer conducted interviews with thirty-one Jewish store owners and their family members, creating over sixty hours of oral history and documenting 454 Jewish-owned stores during a 110-year period. Some family stories went back to the late 1800s. After the railroad came through the mountains at Old Fort in 1879 and reached Asheville by 1880, a rapid expansion of Asheville's population included many Jewish families who were, like others, attracted by the opportunities of a growing community and the health benefits of the mountains.

The interviewees told of the early struggles their families faced, the challenges of running a family business and their experiences growing up Jewish in a predominantly Christian culture. Although a few told of minor incidents of prejudice, most believed their families were accepted as part of their communities.

Here is an excerpt from the interview with Trudy Schwarzberg Packard:

> *Uncle S.H. [Michalove]—this is a very interesting story—you know, when they first came to Asheville, they didn't just have a store...They used to peddle—they used to go on the road and sell their wares to people on the farms and in the country.*
>
> *And when Uncle S.H. went out, he had a few cups and saucers and things, just odd things...that he put on the wagon, and these ladies on the farm or whatever places where he visited, they went for all these dishes and all these things. And they didn't go for the apparel, because there were so many of them traveling with it, that he thought, you know, this [dishware] would be a good field maybe.*
>
> *So he would get more and more—I don't know where he imported it from, probably Baltimore—like everything came from Baltimore at that time. And he would do that. And finally, he ended up opening up a little store in Asheville, and then a bigger store and then a bigger store. And it became, really, really a showplace in Asheville.*

Here is an excerpt from the interview with Betty Pollack Golden:

> *Q. So when did he open up his shoe store? [Lou Pollock—Globe Shoes]*
> *A. I think it was in the middle 1920s. He started this Christmas party deal...he says he wants to give shoes away, so he started working with the churches and with the Salvation Army; and he counted how many shoes he wanted to do that year, when he first started. And they got the most*

needy children, and they brought them there. And then it grew. They had so many children, and he never turned anybody away. It became a real special thing for this Jewish man, who was having this Christmas party for children that needed shoes.

Daddy had helpers there that you wouldn't believe. He had judges that came in, lawyers that came, some from the police department and the nuns from St. Genevieve…anybody that wanted to come…My father would have all these children seated, and he would go down and say 3-B, 6-A, 2-B—and he named what size they needed. He had all these shoes up there, and they would get them.

Most of them were wearing the ones from the year before that they got there—and if they had holes in them, he took them away from them. If they didn't, and they were OK, he would put new laces in, and they would put them over their shoulder and wear their new shoes out. And at the end of the day, he had taken all these shoes that were just of no use—and they had started piling them up, piling them up. And it looked like a big Christmas tree, when they got all through. And it was quite a stunning sight to see.

➺ ⋘

THE PROJECT EVOLVES

Using highlights from the interviews, Schochet and Fahrer created a public display consisting of twelve three- by five-foot panels titled *The Family Store: A History of the Jewish Businesses of Downtown Asheville, 1880–1990*. The exhibit panels were printed on a special material that could be rolled up and easily transported. Initially displayed in downtown storefronts, they became the focus of a walking tour in Asheville.

> You kind of have this one little idea, and then, in the end it is so much different and so much bigger than you ever really thought it would be.
> —Jan Schochet

The panels represent a small portion of the information collected, but they provided a powerful way to share it with the public, using photographs, maps and excerpts from newspaper articles, letters and store records. Each panel featured a street, an iconic store, a person or a family that made a major contribution to Asheville's history.

The Family Store: A History Of Jewish Businesses In Downtown Asheville, 1880–1990

Every town has its legendary businesses and The Man Store was certainly one of those. Most people who lived in or anywhere near Asheville from 1922 until the store left downtown in the early 1970s were familiar with it. Coleman Zageir (1894-1975) opened The Man Store in 1922 and operated it for more than forty years at the same location, 22 Patton Avenue. The Man Store was sold to Hart, Schaffner & Marx in 1963. It eventually moved to the Asheville Mall, underwent a name change and closed.

Coleman Zageir

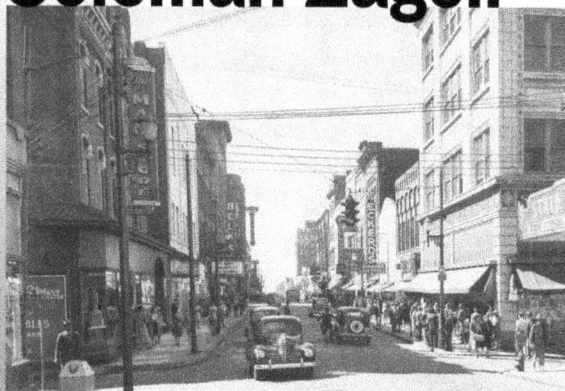

He was a modest man, stating, "If you are a member of the community, that's a responsibility you should recognize and assume." Yet he disliked publicity and only gave three interviews to the media in his lifetime. His service was recognized by the University of North Carolina at Asheville when one of its new classroom buildings was named Coleman Zageir Social Sciences Building in 1974.

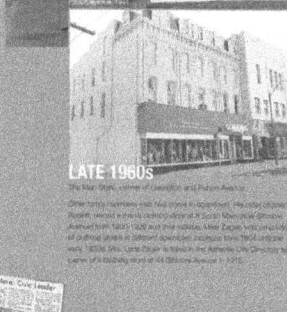

LATE 1960s

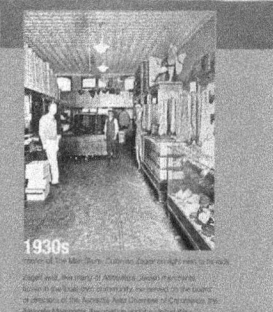

1930s

An Unsung Hero...

"Coleman always chewed a cigar. He never lit it – he chewed it all the time. Kind of an old thing... He just had a way of making people feel special.

And my daddy didn't have any money... He owned a funeral home in Bryson City. So we'd go over [to Asheville] and he would refinance a vehicle at Wachovia [Bank]... and then he would go down and pay Coleman Zageir for what he bought the year before, and then he would buy whole new outfits for the coming year...

He was always out jur behind with Coleman. But [Coleman] didn't care, because he knew daddy was good for it and was always going to show up around Christmas time. Kind of a neat thing."
— Reg Moody
Owner, Moody's Funeral Home, Sylva, NC

"I loved that man. I got my first suit there when i was twelve. He sheen in a shirt and a tie for five. He had no far life."
— Chan Gordon
Owner, The Captain's Bookshelf, Asheville

"I had graduated from high school and was accepted at Asheville-Biltmore College [now UNC-A] and I did not own a suit. I wanted one for college. So I went to The Man Store to buy one. I had on a beautiful tan summer suit and the tailor was marking the pants length while I stood in front of the three-way mirror. And Mr. Zageir walked by. And he stopped and he looked at me in that suit. He said something to the salesman, who answered him back.

'And he came over and said to me, 'You shoulder is higher than the other. We need to cut the padding down.' And he told that shelk from the tailor and he

marked up the shoulder with it. He was walking all around me marking up that suit. His hands were just flying with that shalk. It was a twenty-six dollar suit. He had hundred dollar suits in his store. But he was treating me like I was one of his best customers. And when I got that suit, it looked wonderful me. I had it for years.

'And I know why he did it—he wanted me to buy all my suits there. The salesman told him it was my first suit and he wanted it to fit me like a custom-tailored suit. He treated me like a millionaire and I know a lot of other men had the exact same experience. I always bought my suits at The Man Store."
— Jim Illy
U.S. Post Office, retired.
Head, Stevulig on the Green, retired, Asheville

"One of Asheville's now prominent doctors came out of the service following World War II hoping to set up practice. It would be a costly venture for this young physician who had little more than the uniform he came home with ... The young doctor dropped in and told Coleman his problem. He didn't have a practice, but was determined to establish one. Mr. Zageir quietly smiled and proceeded to outfit the young doctor. No bill was ever mailed. A simple oral statement at the doctor left: 'When you can.' Four years later the debt was paid. There were many others who received similar help in launching their careers."
— Arthur Whiteside, Editorial Director, WLOG-TV
Delivered on WLOG upon death of Coleman Zageir
Daily Advisory for Dec. 4, 1975

The Family Store: A History of Jewish Businesses. Copyright History@Hand; courtesy of Jan Schochet and Sharon Fahrer.

An accompanying brochure titled *The Family Store* described each panel and contained a map with all the locations. The public responded with enthusiasm, and merchants liked the increased traffic as people came by to see the display and pick up a brochure. The exhibit won the prestigious Griffin Award from the Preservation Society of Asheville and Buncombe County.

Fahrer and Schochet recall that when the panels were on display, several people called to thank them for doing the exhibit, as it brought back a lot of memories of people and places from the time when downtown was a vibrant shopping hub.

The panels were later moved to other locations, including Pack Place and the Beth Ha-Tephila congregation in Asheville. One panel remains as a permanent display at the corner of Patton and Lexington Avenues, where the Man Store was once located.

The D.H. Ramsey Library at UNC-Asheville now houses the audios, documents and photos collected in the research. Additional grants enabled the library to digitize not only the Family Store project but also its other collections of historical information documenting over a century of Jewish life in the Asheville area. This rich history is now accessible to anyone with a computer.

Knowing our history helps us understand and appreciate what we have as a community. Those who came before us laid the foundation on which we have built our own lives, and their lives help inform who we are today. These stories were missing pieces in our understanding of the history of Asheville, and they add to the richness of our heritage.

❧ ❦

You have to know where you came from to know where you're going.
—Sharon Fahrer

❧ ❦

What We Learned

Two people, with passion and determination, can turn a personal interest into a project benefiting an entire community.

FROM THE HARRY WINNER PANEL

As he began to modernize his store in the 1960s, he realized that adding an automated elevator would cost the elevator operator her job. He asked her to become a salesclerk. He arranged for other department stores to hire African American salespeople, who would begin working on the same day in order to integrate their sales forces simultaneously and in a low-key way. His wife, Julienne, said recently, "He did it because he knew it was the right thing to do."

CONTINUING THE WORK

Sharon Fahrer, through History@Hand, continued the research begun for the Family Store project and has created several other interpretive panels, including displays for several of the buildings at UNC-Asheville, honoring the men—many of them Jewish store owners—whose financial contributions enabled the university to grow. The history of the Asheville Jewish community is commemorated in panels for Beth Ha-Tephila and Beth Israel congregations and the Jewish Community Center. Other panels honor individuals such as author Wilma Dykeman and physician and philanthropist Sprinza Weizenblatt.

10

YMI AND THE BLOCK

Growth and Revival of a Community Center

If we keep the right mix of residences, businesses, arts and entertainment and be mindful of the spiritual and environmental aspects of community, we will have a much healthier, [more] resilient community that can sustain itself.
—Stephanie Swepson-Twitty

In 1889, George Washington Vanderbilt II, son of railroad magnate William Henry Vanderbilt, bought a large tract of land near Asheville and set about to build a home. About that time, the increase in tourism and the growth of the hospitality industry had spawned a proliferation of saloons and houses of prostitution. These two factors laid the groundwork for a collaboration that would have a far-reaching impact on the history of Asheville.

The Black leaders in Asheville were concerned about the moral atmosphere in the area. Wanting to create programs that would offer a positive alternative for young Black men and help them gain respectability in the white population, some of the men attempted to start a Young Men's Christian Association (YMCA) but could not raise the necessary funds.

They hoped that as Blacks developed character that was more in line with white Americans, character traits that were reflective of the Victorian ethos of the late nineteenth century, whites would be more inclined to view them as worthy of their full rights as citizens.
—Darin Waters

The YMI building, 2015. *Photo by Nancy Orban.*

In 1892, two of the Black leaders, Isaac Dickson and Edward Stephens, approached Vanderbilt to ask for a loan to enable them to buy the land and construct a building that would be an attractive gathering place for the young men. By then, their vision had expanded to creating a place where men could come for education, as well as to enrich their social, cultural and business lives.

As there were many Black men employed as construction workers on Vanderbilt's new house, he took an interest in their well-being and wanted to help with the development of a community center. Vanderbilt agreed to a loan of $15,000, but he actually invested $23,000 in the land and construction of the building that would become the Young Men's Institute (YMI). The eighteen-thousand-square-foot building was designed by Richard Sharp Smith, a resident architect at what would be known as the Biltmore Estate, with input from the local Black leaders. Construction began in 1892 and was completed in 1893.

The YMI's organizers expected the businesses renting space in the building, along with membership fees, to provide a reliable, ongoing source of income to defray operating expenses and create a fund to repay the loan.

Vanderbilt held the title to the land and building until the loan was repaid. For the first thirteen years, he paid for maintenance, insurance and upkeep of the building. He also paid the salaries of the general secretary, the executive director, the custodian and the kindergarten teacher.

AT THE CENTER OF IT ALL

Located at the corner of Eagle and Market Streets in downtown Asheville, the YMI quickly became a community center at the heart of the Black community. It had meeting space for lectures or community events, a well-stocked library and reading rooms, classrooms, a fully equipped gymnasium and a swimming pool. Space on the ground floor was set aside for retail and other businesses, and soon a doctor's office, a drugstore and other businesses were serving the public.

Academic programs emphasized liberal arts as well as practical skills. They included a kindergarten, an industrial school, night schools, a domestic arts school and a normal school offering classes in reading, spelling, grammar, arithmetic, geography, history, science and writing. In the second year, students could study algebra, geometry, natural philosophy and chemistry.

> Instead of just a place where the city's Black men could gather for social and moral edification, the YMI became a social, cultural and economic incubator for the entire Black community...At the YMI, Asheville's Black residents were able to interact, think and create more freely than they might have been in other places.
> —Darin Waters

The YMI offered musical performances by its own chorus and band, and sometimes it was able to draw artists from outside the region. It also sponsored lectures by local leaders and accomplished professionals and invited prominent Black leaders to speak for its annual lecture series.

Membership was available to anyone for a fee, and some white neighbors joined the institute. Black workers at the Biltmore Estate were required to purchase a membership, but most other Black workers were employed in low-wage jobs and few were able to afford memberships. Almost half of the Black workers in the area were employed in service positions in hotels, boardinghouses and sanatoriums. As the area drew more tourists and new residents, many

The YMI orchestra, 1908. *Courtesy of (p77.10.3.8.1a) Black Highlanders Collection, circa 1888–1972, D.H. Ramsey Library, Special Collections, University of North Carolina at Asheville 28804.*

Black men were employed as construction workers, helping to build the hotels, commercial buildings and homes required to meet the demands of growth.

At the same time, a few Black entrepreneurs were starting businesses to offer the goods and services not available to Black customers from white businesses. These included barbershops, grocery stores, a bank, an insurance company, a drugstore, two funeral homes and several restaurants. Many of these businesses, like the YMI, were located along Eagle and Market Streets, which came to be known as "The Block."

Vanderbilt continued to provide financial support to the YMI until 1906. At that time, he asked for repayment of only $10,000 of the original loan. With help from their members and from the larger community, the YMI organizers were able to raise the money and buy the title to the building. With the YMI at its heart, The Block became the Black business center in Asheville, and it continued to grow and thrive alongside the neighborhood that grew up around it, which came to be known as East End. Even during and after the Great Depression, The Block continued to serve as the Black financial center in Asheville.

FAST-FORWARD TO 2015

❯·❮

The woman eases into a chair by the window of the café on Market Street. She sips her coffee and looks out the window to the building under construction across the street. She feels a surge of excitement at the realization that she and her daughter and two grandchildren will soon be moving into one of the beautiful apartments in that building. It has been a long journey, but it is finally coming full circle.

Her mind goes back to her childhood, when she lived in one of the houses on the hill not far from here. She has fond memories of coming to this very building after school to use the library. So many memories flood back—laughing on the way to school with her brother, getting ice cream on Saturdays with her friends, going to the doctor when she was sick... She stops herself.

This is a time to be grateful for the present and what the future holds. She looks out again at the building across the way. She's heard that it will have a playground for the grandchildren and a beautiful courtyard right in the middle of the building. She's worked hard to raise her daughter and grandchildren, and now—soon—they will be returning to the place that nurtured her when she was growing up. It's changed a lot, but there is a new energy of expectation and hope for the future. She's glad to be coming back home.

❯·❮

With the energy provided by new collaborations, The Block is coming back from the decades of decline that followed urban renewal in Asheville in the 1970s. Leading the revitalization movement is Eagle Market Streets Development Corporation (EMSDC), a not-for-profit organization whose vision is "to bring the opportunity for economic and social independence to the low-to-moderate-income community." Three programs have emerged from that vision, and they lay the groundwork for others to follow.

INDIVIDUAL DEVELOPMENT ACCOUNTS

With a goal of empowering individuals to improve their lives, EMSDC entered into a partnership with the North Carolina Department of Labor to create the Individual Development Account for Business Development program. The program is designed to help individuals develop good financial habits while they are taking the first step in building their personal assets and creating financial independence.

Participants deposit an agreed-upon amount into their account each month, and when their account reaches $1,000, they receive a four-to-one match, giving them $5,000 of seed money to invest in their education or job training or to help them begin a business. Along the way, they also receive money management training that includes budgeting, cleaning up a credit score and following a savings schedule.

EAGLE MARKET PLACE COMMUNITY

> That will be the legacy we leave—how we solved the challenge of two things, economics and housing.
> —Stephanie Swepson-Twitty

This planned, mixed-use development is coming into being as a result of the collaboration of two major not-for-profit corporations: Eagle Market Streets Development Corporation, a primarily Black organization, and Mountain Housing Opportunities, a primarily white organization. This fifty/fifty partnership is creating a major community asset in the middle of The Block that will help meet the need for affordable housing and add a major economic stimulus to the area.

Eagle Market Place will provide sixty-two affordable workforce apartments, over six thousand square feet of community/multi-use space and over seven thousand square feet of commercial, retail and office space. The residential site will include an indoor playground, a fitness center, a computer center, a youth center, a large community room and an interior courtyard.

All of this will emerge from the renovation of three historic buildings—the Del Cardo building, the Dr. Collette building and the Ritz building—and the construction of one new building. When completed, the project will include over ninety-two thousand square feet, all built to Energy Star standards. It is made possible by funding from both public and private sources, including the City of Asheville.

BLOCK-BY-BLOCK INDUSTRIES

Eagle Market Streets' signature workforce development program offers design/development entrepreneurs an opportunity to have their prototype/ samples produced in America and in a local environment. One early program trains individuals in the trade of commercial production sewing.

THE RETURN OF A COMMUNITY

The YMI is still at the heart of The Block. After decades of struggle, it is slowly reclaiming its role as a community gathering place. With a focus on education, arts and entertainment, it is inviting community organizations and programs to use its ample space for performances, public forums and other events. As businesses once again locate in the building, they will bring more people and new energy to the YMI.

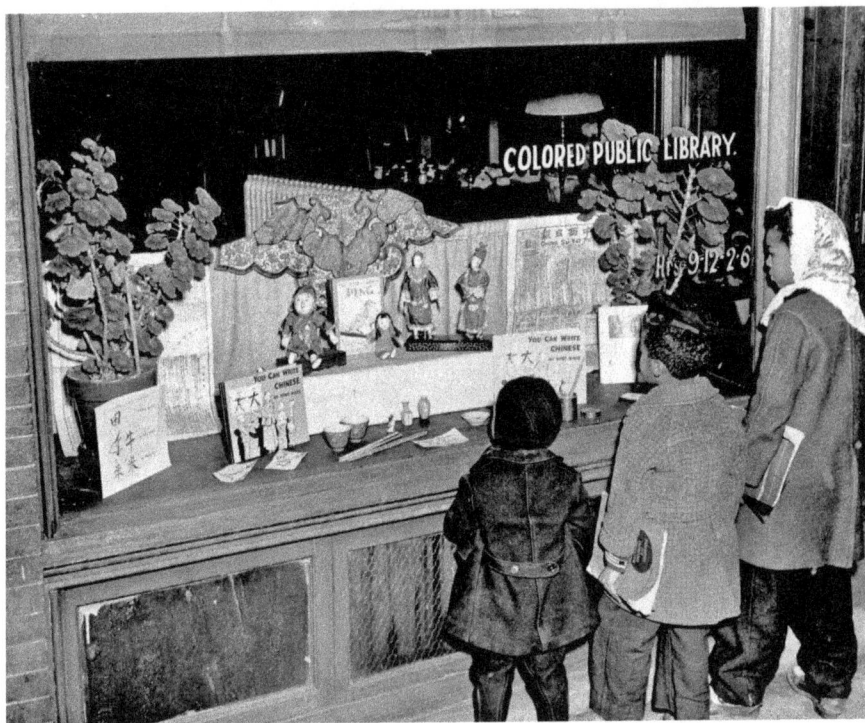

The Colored Public Library at YMI, circa 1945–51. *Courtesy of Pack Memorial Library.*

These developments are a major step in returning The Block to the vibrant, resilient area it once was. More than buildings are being built or renovated—there is also a spirit of caring for one another, of being part of a greater whole. That is what community is all about.

>> <<

What we want to be is community,
and a true community counts all of us.
—Stephanie Swepson-Twitty

>> <<

WHAT WE LEARNED

Community building is an ongoing process. We cannot recapture the past, but often, we can recapture a vision and build on what has gone before.

MISSION

Eagle Market Streets' mission is to develop people, property and businesses, and it envisions economic and social justice for all.

VISION

Guided by our mission, EMSDC's vision is to bring the opportunity for economic and social independence to the low- to moderate-income community. It focuses on property development, economic business and workforce development.

CORE VALUES

EMSDC envisions a sustainable, just and promising community where minority and underserved populations are elevated from poverty by means of:

- opportunity
- economic and social independence
- empowerment
- self-sufficiency
- asset and wealth building
- social entrepreneurship
- education
- awareness

THE MAGIC OF COLLABORATION

Heroes are not giant statues framed against a red sky.
They are people who say, "This is my community,
and it is my responsibility to make it better."
—Studs Terkel

The collaboration process changes people and often transforms communities. When we collaborate to meet a challenge or address a need, something almost magical happens. It begins with a belief in the possibilities, and through the synergy of different minds and intentions coming together with a shared purpose, a solution often emerges that none alone could have imagined—a result that is so much richer and deeper because of the unique contribution of each person.

If these stories have inspired you, I encourage you to consider how you can begin a collaborative project. Think of it as an adventure that will enrich your life. Are you concerned about a need in your community that is not being addressed? Are you a business owner who could cooperate with your competitors in a way that supports all of you and serves the community at the same time? Do you have a passionate interest that you would like to pursue? Is it important enough to you to take the first step and find others who share your concern?

THE IMPORTANCE OF LEADERSHIP

Another factor of successful collaboration is that you've got people who are willing to be leaders and take the ball and run with it.
—Jill Jones

Sometimes leaders show up at the beginning with a vision and enough passion to bring others on board and see it through to completion. Sometimes leaders emerge from the process. When Wayne Caldwell saw his family's business threatened by the proposed downtown mall project, he gathered others, and under his leadership, they created Save Downtown Asheville. For almost two years, he showed up at every public hearing that involved the mall project and argued for the preservation of the city he loved.

Becky Anderson saw the opportunity in a request for proposals and led the effort to obtain a grant against huge odds. She then went on as director of HandMade in America to take her collaborative skills to the small towns of Western North Carolina, where she and her staff and volunteers empowered local people to create their own collaborations for the betterment of their communities.

When Brian and Gail McCarthy bought Highwater Clays, they intended to create a reliable family income. Over time, the vision of a community of artists came alive, and they emerged as trailblazers, leading the way to what would become the River Arts District.

Dick Gilbert saw the potential for some empty buildings, and he became the guiding light of the Friends, who were a force for good in the community for many years. Betty and David Huskins, with experience from High Country Host, saw the need for a similar collaboration in the far western counties of the state, and they led the effort to create Smoky Mountain Host.

When Toby Ives stepped into the directorship of MANNA Food Bank, he quickly adopted the MANNA vision and worked tirelessly for years to bring it to reality.

Sharing a passion for service and a belief in the power of cooperation, Angie Chandler and Jill Jones stepped into leadership positions at Blue Ridge National Heritage Area and helped people in dozens of towns in the region protect and develop their heritage assets. In the process, they empowered many others to take on leadership roles in their own towns.

Sharing the Vision

Get your vision and go out and sell it.
—Brett D. Miller

Give people an opportunity to help. Be open about what you are doing. Open your mouth and don't think you can do it yourself... You might actually find the vein of gold you didn't know was there.
—Jan Schochet

We don't have to do it alone. A few people can launch a project that will have a huge impact on a larger community. The shared desire to be in service to others can be the driving force of a powerful collaboration.

Who else cares about the issue that concerns you? Who are the stakeholders? Who would be impacted by the project? Who may have insights into the problem or perhaps hold a key to a creative solution? How can you bring them on board? The answers will be different in every situation.

MANNA Food Bank grew from the meeting of a few people whose clients experienced ongoing hunger, and it grew into a region-wide program that serves thousands of people through a network of over two hundred organizations.

The Family Store project arose from a personal interest shared by two people. They found others who shared their interest and helped them to document an important part of the history of a city.

Smoky Mountain Host and the Great Smoky Mountains Golf Association found their partners among their competitors, and they learned how to work together for the benefit of all. In the process, they all prospered and a regional economy expanded.

Do you know one or two people who share your interest? Begin the conversation, and you may be surprised where it leads you.

Finding Common Ground

There's always talking to the choir... but that's not who you want to talk to. If you're going to make something a real community project, you have to go out there and try to reach the people who aren't the choir.
—Sharon Fahrer

The challenge was to get them to see the value of working together and to come to the table and let go of their politics and their deals, so they could see that it's time to start talking.
—Angie Chandler

Be sure to invite anyone to join you who may have an insight into the problem or a creative idea for a solution. When you get all the stakeholders together on any project, however, you are likely to encounter disagreements and conflicts. The key to success is to help them find common ground.

When HandMade in America and the Blue Ridge National Heritage Area staff brought local volunteers together in a planning process, many of the people at the table had never spoken to one another, seeming to have nothing in common. In the end, they discovered a shared purpose and joined forces to create projects that transformed the economy and enriched the local culture.

The folks at Save Downtown Asheville teamed up with a group that didn't really care very much about saving the city center but was passionately opposed to more taxes. These two diverse intentions coming together for a common purpose led to a successful coalition.

Even with a shared interest, people often have conflicting ideas about the solution. The best results arise from a good old-fashioned brainstorming session in which everyone has a voice and all ideas are respected and considered, even ideas that seem, at first, to be wild and crazy.

USING ALL AVAILABLE RESOURCES

You can't just say "Let's have a meeting and let's collaborate." That's great, but once you collaborate, there's got to be some way of bringing resources to the table to help get the work done.
—Jill Jones

What resources—ideas, money, service organizations, government, media, people, buildings, equipment—are available that can support your project?

The founders of MANNA Food Bank located a free space to begin their project and recruited volunteers to approach businesses for food and money. They also began a business that supported a local grocery store chain, and in exchange, they earned money while they secured food that otherwise would have been wasted.

The leaders of Smoky Mountain Host became involved in the political process and secured state funding for marketing.

Friends Enterprises launched Stone Soup in some old buildings that were not being used and created a for-profit business to support its work in the community.

HandMade in America and the Blue Ridge National Heritage Area relied on grant funding and hundreds of volunteers to carry out their missions.

Deserted warehouses and industrial buildings along the river provided the ideal spawning ground for a community of artists who needed affordable studio spaces, and slowly, the River Arts District came to life.

The Family Store project was launched with the support of the university, the local library and scholars from around the state. Grants and local contributions funded the process.

The idea of wrapping eleven acres of downtown Asheville in donated fabric to demonstrate the extent of the planned destruction seemed totally unrealistic, but it resulted in a powerful demonstration that provided the first step in altering the proposed course of history for the city.

The Black leaders in Asheville in the 1890s needed funding to provide a community center that would support their young men. There were very few resources available to them at that time, so they took the bold move of asking George Vanderbilt for his help, and he became their partner in the YMI.

Is there a resource in your community not being used—a piece of land in neglect or an empty building? How can it support your project? What about people resources—professionals who would be willing to donate some time and offer their skills or retired folks who would enjoy making a contribution? Who might have a creative idea that would help move you forward? How can you recruit others to join you? Local media will welcome your story, and many groups are looking for interesting speakers. Be creative and be bold!

PATIENCE AND LEARNING AS YOU GO

No one came with a blueprint—we learned as we went.
There were things we just learned from doing.
—Carolyn Wallace

We forget things take time. You want to change a
community—it doesn't happen overnight.
—Becky Anderson

The early supporters of **MANNA** Food Bank knew nothing about running a food bank, and they received no early support from the local food industry, but they learned as they went. They recruited a small force of volunteers who cared enough about the hunger issue to go out and start talking to businesses. Years later, this regional collaboration serves people in sixteen counties.

When HandMade in America was launched, the task seemed overwhelming—how to get local citizens in dozens of small towns to come together and develop a plan for their communities. They began with a months-long planning process that included representatives from each town. The next step evolved out of the first—getting local citizens on board in each local area. The process took years, and they learned as they went. The resulting regional collaboration led to significant economic growth and a new regional identity among towns that had previously been disconnected from one another.

The Save Downtown Asheville folks had no idea how they were going to fight the powerful forces behind the mall project, but they had a passionate love for their city. For almost two years, they took action in every way they could think of, and they prevailed against the odds.

These people did not give up when things didn't come together quickly. They kept learning and looking for new ways to bring others on board. Any new venture requires patience, commitment and not giving up when the going gets rough.

SUPPORTING EVERYONE'S INTERESTS

These folks all had a business interest—they all had skin in
the game. You have to ask the "What's in it for them?"
question, and the answer was the dollars.
—Mark Singleton

The purpose of collaborating is to support diverse interests. People
have preferences, and if all are available, everyone benefits.
—Joe Eckert

Perhaps the most challenging collaboration is one where you ask competitors to join forces for their mutual benefit. In such a case, cooperation seems counterintuitive. Before joining Smoky Mountain Host or the Great Smoky Mountains Golf Association, members had to be shown how participating in the collaboration would help their individual businesses. Then they were on board.

Asheville provides many other examples of cooperation among competitors, including Asheville Independent Restaurants and Asheville Brewers Alliance, which present a unified invitation to tourists to enjoy the many diverse dining and drinking experiences the city offers.

In each case, a few people had a vision of how it would work, and one by one, they sold the idea to the more skeptical. By working together, they reached a larger audience and attracted more customers to the area.

TAKING ACTION BEFORE YOU KNOW WHERE IT WILL TAKE YOU

Start with a concept. As you pursue it, someone has an idea. Other ideas come, and you create a web, with no concept of where it will go. In the end, it is so different and so much bigger than you ever really thought it would be.
—Jan Schochet

You do not have to know the end result or how you are going to get there. It's OK to begin a cooperative venture and learn as you go. Most collaborative projects unfold in unanticipated ways.

When Jan Schochet and Sharon Fahrer set out to research the lives of Jewish store owners in Asheville, they didn't know that their project would evolve into a series of interpretive panels that tell the stories of people who helped shape a city.

The Friends who began Stone Soup intended to support a group of nonprofit agencies. They didn't see the other ways in which they would later serve the larger community.

Each new person or idea brings the possibility of a new direction, and each addition contributes to the richness of the final result.

RISING TO THE CHALLENGE

Remind people they are valuable—and by empowering them to take action, you are showing them they are, and they rise to the occasion.
—Becky Anderson

Above all, the process of collaboration changes us. It demands a lot from us and often brings out our best self as we work together to solve a problem or to create something new. It teaches us to listen to and respect the ideas of others and to see their needs as important as our own. It requires us to reach inside and access our deeper wisdom and creativity. In the end, we see the magic of collaboration comes from within us, and we are transformed in the process.

❖ ❖

Believe in synergy. Believe that if we really do collaborate, what we come out with will be far better than any great idea that any one or two or three of us could ever have.
—Carolyn Wallace

INDEX

ABOUT THE AUTHOR

In 1977, Marilyn Ball moved to the Asheville area as part of a wave of newcomers who were learning to live self-sufficiently in the spirit of community. Through the years, working together with many of the region's community leaders and visionaries, Ball helped formulate collaborative initiatives for Western North Carolina's emerging tourism, hospitality and economic development industries.

Photo by Greg Miller.

By bringing a range of resources to the same table, she fostered a spirit of mutual cooperation and purpose and helped diverse groups establish more effective and focused strategies to achieve their individual and collective goals. In the process, she accumulated a wealth of knowledge about the area's history and gained a deep respect for collaboration and how working together helps create community.